North East and Cumbria NHS Libraries

NEC00002

659.2934

WX
228
HEA

KU-362-597

Health Service Public Relations

A guide to good practice

Second Edition

Edited by **Roger Silver**

Published on behalf of

**National Association of Health
Service Public Relations Officers**

Radcliffe Medical Press • Oxford and New York

© 1995 Roger Silver

Radcliffe Medical Press Ltd
18 Marcham Road, Abingdon, Oxon, OX14 1AA, UK

Radcliffe Medical Press, Inc.
141 Fifth Avenue, New York, NY 10010, USA

All rights reserved. No part of this publication may be reproduced, stored in a retrieval system, or transmitted, in any form or by any means, electronic, mechanical, photocopying, recording or otherwise without the prior permission of the copyright owner.

British Library Cataloguing in Publication Data

A catalogue record for this book is available from the British Library.

ISBN 1 85775 028 4

Library of Congress Cataloging-in-Publication Data is available.

CLASS ✓
WX
228
HEA

ACC
508068

EAST CUMBRIA
EDUCATION CENTRE
LIBRARY

Typeset by Multiplex medway limited, Walderslade, Kent
Printed and bound in Great Britain by Biddles Ltd, Guildford and King's Lynn

Contents

List of contributors

Tim Albert, Consultant and Trainer in Written Communication; formerly Editor, *BMA News Review*

Peter Campion, Public Relations Manager, Southampton University Hospitals NHS Trust, Southampton

Jim Clayton, Public Relations Consultant, Jim Clayton Associates; formerly Regional Public Relations Manager, West Midlands Regional Health Authority, Birmingham

Tim Clegg, Head of Communications, Tamworth Borough Council; formerly Head of Corporate Affairs, South Durham Health Authority, Durham

Rob Dalton, Head of Public Affairs, South and West Regional Health Authority, Winchester

Bill Gillespie, Director of Communications, South Thames Regional Health Authority, London

Richard Green, Acting Communications Manager, South and West Regional Health Authority, Bristol

Jane Kerr, Press and Public Relations Manager, The Royal Berkshire and Battle Hospitals NHS Trust, Reading

Terry Linehan, Director, Insight Management Solutions, Dorchester

Andrew Moss, Manager, Oxford Health Public Relations, Oxford

Andrew Partington, Communications Manager, East Sussex Health Authority, Eastbourne; Chairman, National Association of Health Service Public Relations Officers

Mark Purcell, Deputy Head of Press and PR, North Thames Regional Health Authority, London

Jennifer Rogers, Public Relations Manager, Chelsea and Westminster Hospitals NHS Trust, London

Linda Rolf, Public Relations Consultant; formerly Regional Public Relations Manager, South West Thames Regional Health Authority, London

Roger Silver, Communications Consultant; formerly Director of Communications, South West Thames Regional Health Authority, London

Jenny Sironis, Press and Communications Manager, Forest Healthcare NHS Trust, Woodford Green, Essex

Jonathan Street, Head of Press and PR, North Thames Regional Health Authority, London

Sue Trimingham, Press and Public Relations Manager, South Downs Health NHS Trust, Brighton

Ian West, Managing Director, HRO'c Design Limited, Birmingham

Ian Wylie, Head of Communications, King's Fund, London

Most of the contributors are members of the National Association of Health Service Public Relations Officers (NAHSPRO). Others have close links with the Association's work.

NAHSPRO is especially grateful to Tim Albert, of Tim Albert and Associates, Leatherhead (the author of Chapter 5, *Writing to be read*), Terry Linehan, of Insight Management Solutions, Dorchester (Chapter 8, *Research and evaluation*) and Ian West, of HRO'c Design Limited, Birmingham (*Graphic design and print*, Chapter 7).

Preface

This book has been produced partly in response to continuing demand for a previous edition published by the King's Fund, London, in 1985. It has been revised to take account of the sweeping changes in health service organization since then, and of the importance now attached to internal and external communications.

Health Service Public Relations has been written principally for health service managers. This means managers in the broadest sense, encompassing not only those people whose jobs carry the title but those who plan, manage and provide health care at every level – from health service board rooms to clinics and wards. It will, we hope, be of use to health care professionals working face to face with patients, as well as managers in policy-forming and decision-making roles, such as chairmen and executive and non-executive members of health authorities and trusts. (The term 'health authorities' is normally used throughout the book to cover district health authorities, family health services authorities and health commissions.)

Like its predecessor, *Health Service Public Relations* is a practical book. It shows how order can be brought into communications through the use of public relations skills and techniques. It is partly intended for dipping into when needed. Therefore, some of the advice and suggestions for dealing with a particular situation – from handling a problem with the news media to putting together an exhibition – are repeated in separate chapters.

Anyone looking for discussion of the impact of advanced electronic technologies on public relations may be disappointed. The book recognizes of course, that the word processor has overtaken the typewriter and that, in today's global village, news and information travel faster than ever. But the fundamental principles and practice of good public relations remain largely unaffected, and for many years individuals and local communities will continue to rely for information and communication on the long-established methods set out in the book.

One of the book's most important chapters, *Research and evaluation*, is to be found at the end. Arguably, it should be right up front. But in many ways this book is like a toolbox. Exploring the contents of a toolbox for the first time, a person may need to know what the tools are for, and how they work, before deciding on the situations in which to use them with the greatest economy and to the maximum benefit.

The contributors are public relations specialists from the NHS and other practitioners with extensive experience of the health service. The editor has drawn freely from the previous edition of *Health Service Public Relations* and is grateful to the King's Fund for permission to do so.

If you need more help on a communications problem or opportunity, we suggest you get in touch with the public relations or communications department at your health authority, trust, or regional office of the NHS Executive, who will do their best to advise you. Failing that, contact Andrew Partington of the National Association of Health Service Public Relations Officers (NAHSPRO), on 01323 520000. The Association will be glad to point you towards the right people.

1

Public relations – for planned communication

Public relations is about planned and deliberate communication. In the complex and rapidly changing world of health care, any organization which fails to communicate in planned and deliberate ways may leave patients, public, staff and opinion formers confused, angry or without confidence in its work.

The first edition of this book stressed that public relations involves a determined responsibility to think, listen, inform, explain, discuss and act in the interests of the people served by an organization. It added that the responsibility becomes a duty and moral obligation in the NHS, which is paid for by the public through taxes and deals with people needing help, often when they are at their most vulnerable.

Nine years and two radical health service reorganizations later, that truth remains. But on the way something significant happened: health service reformers and managers discovered Communications. Historians of the NHS will place the discovery somewhere between the Age of Quality Assurance and the Dawn of Corporate Governance. Taking a longer view, they may record that many were so exhilarated by what they had found that they fell into a trap recognized 300 years earlier by John Locke in *An essay concerning human understanding*:

> 'Another abuse of Language is an affected Obscurity, by applying old Words to new and unusual Significations; or introducing new and ambiguous Terms without defining either; or else putting them so together as may confound their ordinary meaning.'

The historians may go on to wonder what Locke would have made of the press statement from a hospital trust, which said:

> 'We operate a Block Contract on behalf of the DHA and it is funded on the assumption that the patient case mix will not change dramatically. Unfortunately, to date, the "medical" specialty element…has,

and continues to squeeze the "surgical" specialty element. In addition, we are over contract on ITU/CCU by 165 bed days.'

Or, from the minutes of a district health authority:

'Provided the financial pressure upon the ECR budget is successfully resolved, through the plans in hand to defer treatments electively in certain areas, an initial year-end surplus of £70000 is currently forecast. Due to an increase over plan for level of ECR cases, activity is currently forecast to be 550 episodes higher at outturn.'

It was not only jargon that sometimes got out of hand. In the communications explosion that followed the 1990 reforms of the NHS, self-congratulatory glossy publications gushed forth on a tide of enthusiasm and optimism from nearly every corner of the newly organized service. The euphoria was eventually tempered by the realities of competition in the internal market (pace Locke), the pressure on finite resources from infinite demands for health and social care, and the challenges of handling change as revolutions in surgery and medicine began to accelerate and affect approaches to health care.

The reforms left the new NHS trusts out of the purview of the Public Bodies (Admission to Meetings) Act 1960, under which statutory health bodies are legally required to conduct the business of their meetings in public. On the other hand, there have been moves towards greater openness in all government and public bodies. The NHS Executive has drafted a code of practice on openness (see Chapter 4) which was the subject of consultation as Health Service Public Relations went to press. The code, which followed the White Paper, Open Government, published in 1993, aims to make sure that people:

- are able to get information about how well the NHS is doing, the cost of services, and the standards of service they can expect

- are given an explanation about any proposed changes to services and the chance to have a say in the decisions made about those changes

- know the reasons for decisions and actions affecting their treatment.

Perhaps one of the most significant communications-related events in health care in the last decade was the freeing of GPs from the ethical constraints that had prevented them from publicizing their services. In 1990, the General Medical Council changed its rules to allow GPs to advertise their services on the grounds that 'good communication between doctors and patients, and between one doctor and another, is fundamental to the provision of good patient care'.

These and other developments, such as the *Patient's Charter* and *The Health of the Nation*, have caused people at every level of health care to think consciously about how they communicate with patients, communities and organizations, how they involve them, and how they forge and maintain alliances – the very essence of public relations.

COMMUNICATIONS – EVERYBODY'S DOING IT

Every day, in countless exchanges, health care professionals and supporting staff are communicating one-to-one with patients, relatives and other users of their services. Hospital and community services, trusts, family doctor practices, primary care teams, health authorities and all the other branches of the vast health service network are communicating with each other, the general public, other agencies, key opinion formers and the news media.

Any of the following may be read, seen or heard to speak for the NHS:

- the Secretary of State

- the Ministers for Health

- the Chief Executive and colleagues on the NHS Executive

- chairmen and executive and non-executive directors of health authorities and commissions

- chairmen and executive and non-executive directors of trusts

- directors of public health

- managers of hospitals and community units

- communications and public relations managers and press officers.

At the same time, many organizations are speaking for the patient. Community health councils are 'patients' watchdogs'; district health authorities are 'people's champions'. Patients are increasingly speaking up for themselves as they become actively involved in decisions about their treatment instead of just being passive recipients of it. They are also being positively encouraged to say how they would like to see services improved.

The communications dimension in health care is thus vast, complex – and largely uncoordinated. The NHS does not easily lend itself to the corporate discipline of most service organizations – the command structure of the police or military, for example, or the rigorously packaged and applied identity of multiple retail chains. The whole health care world is made up of countless millions of pieces of human interaction, in which the process of communication may be long, difficult and incomplete. Meaning and understanding are hard to achieve when messages are difficult or painful, when audiences are diverse, fragmented or worried, or when communication is by third-party media such as print and broadcasting.

There is also the inter-relationship of message, audience and media, enshrined in Marshall McLuhan's phrase, 'In operational and practical fact, the medium is the message'. His central thesis was that any medium of communication is an extension of humanity and necessarily determines behaviour, thinking and thus what we wish to communicate. As patients become more involved in decisions about their own treatment, so the relationship changes between patient and practitioner, and the messages by which health care is delivered also change fundamentally.

That is principally an issue for the messengers – the doctors and their professional colleagues in their confidential, one-to-one clinical relationship with the patient – and, as professionals, they are at liberty to communicate well, indifferently or badly. Except in extreme circumstances demanding intervention, the issue is outside the control of the managers. But it is not outside their influence.

The managers – from the NHS Executive to health authorities and trusts – create the conditions in which the care-givers work. Communicating effectively and constructively with them, with each other and with the public calls for conscious effort if conditions of confusion, conflict and mixed messages are to be avoided. It is especially important if there is not to be a recurrence of the kind of uncivil and well-publicized strife that has broken out from time to time between health service bodies who may have forgotten that they are part of the same national organization.

Communications cannot be left to chance. At a one-to-one level they are difficult enough. In the bustle of the NHS, they can be chaotic unless the managers are clear about with whom they should be communicating, what they should be communicating, how they should be communicating, and to what purpose.

Which is where public relations comes in.

PUBLIC RELATIONS – WHAT IT ISN'T AND WHAT IT IS

Public relations may be seen as a positive force or a negative force. On the negative side, it may be a term of abuse as when the journalist, Malcolm Muggeridge, seeking to reflect the public's distaste for Anthony Eden as Prime Minister, wrote, 'They asked for a leader and were given a public relations officer'.

It may be associated with a packaged event in which the substance of what is happening takes second place to the way it is presented.

It may be a 'public relations disaster' if a carefully crafted image is destroyed by the truth. Gerald Ratner's spontaneous view that some of his products were 'crap', seen in light of the subsequent decline of his business fortune, is a legendary example of a public relations gaffe.

Public relations may be menacing. In a pluralistic society, the control and packaging of information may amount to no more harm than gloss and hyperbole. In a closed society it may take the form of totalitarian control of state information and misinformation.

The positive side of public relations, which is the subject of this book, has been well defined by the Institute of Public Relations:

> 'Public relations practice is the planned and sustained effort to establish and maintain goodwill and mutual understanding between an organization and its publics.'

The Institute adds:

> 'Public relations is about reputation – the result of what you do, what you say and what others say about you.
>
> Public relations practice is the discipline which looks after reputation with the aim of earning understanding and support and influencing opinion and behaviour.'

Every health service organization, from a GP practice to the national Executive, needs to be good at this positive type of public relations, just as it needs to be good at strategic and operational planning, information and financial management, quality control, marketing and customer services. (Indeed, public relations is often a crucial component of marketing and customer services.)

Public relations contributes to the overall success or failure of the general management activity of an organization, and so ultimately to the success or failure of the organization itself. If financial management looks after the money, public relations looks after people. Public relations is about people who work for the organization and those who are connected with it as users, suppliers, regulators, competitors or pundits.

Public relations is the process by which an organization:

- establishes and maintains high-quality communications with people to fulfil its objectives or responsibilities

- analyses communication problems between organizations and audiences, and finds ways to resolve them

- devises and develops the means by which knowledge and understanding flow between organizations and the people who work in them.

Public relations recognizes the dimension and complexity of health service communications and the need for a systematic way of supporting, ordering and improving them. Through public relations, managers are given the means to consider and agree their communications priorities, and act on them.

The public relations process is primarily the responsibility of the people at the top. Sir John Harvey-Jones, management guru and former chairman of ICI, has written that a good company chairman spends his or her time on strategic planning and public relations. The same applies in the health service. Moreover, the process has to start inside the organization.

An organization is not in a position to 'establish and maintain goodwill and mutual understanding' externally if it lacks these qualities in relations with its own staff. Every manager has a responsibility to ensure that staff are kept fully informed about any matters which affect their working conditions, job content and prospects. This is especially important in an organization like the NHS, which is subject to ever-accelerating change.

Staff who are, or feel they are, in the dark about changes rapidly become demoralized. They will not understand change, nor co-operate in it, unless they are informed, consulted and treated in ways which demonstrate that they matter and that what they say and feel matters. Managers must take deliberate steps to ensure that staff understand clearly issues that affect them. If they neglect or fail to do so, staff will turn to other, probably less dependable, sources or rely on hearsay and rumour.

If staff dislike the organization, its reputation will suffer and the confidence of outsiders will be eroded. If staff are proud of their organization and enjoy working in it, they will tell others. Good internal relations are the springboard for good external public relations.

COMMUNICATIONS IN ACTION

Good internal and external public relations will not just happen. There has to be a disciplined approach in which the people at the top of the organization discuss and reach agreement about:

- their most important audiences

- the messages they want to communicate to them

- what they want their audiences to feel and believe

- who should be communicating with whom

- methods they will use to communicate

- the skills and specialist support they will need

- ways to encourage feedback

- how they will handle feedback

- how they will judge and assess their success or failure.

They must also go out and listen to the most important audiences in the community, learning what they think about the organization and the ways it communicates with them. They should find out if those audiences *feel* regarded as highly as the organization actually regards them.

A health authority whose board places the highest importance on GPs may discover that many GPs nevertheless feel that their opinions are disregarded and that they are treated as being of medium importance or less. The reasons may be to do with systems or with behaviour. Either way, damaged bridges may need repairing. There can also be problems if community health councils, the official consumer bodies in the NHS, are merely tolerated by the health authorities. Health authorities, the 'people's champions', and community health councils, the 'patients' watchdogs', must work together productively.

If they want to communicate effectively with their audiences, executive and non-executive board members of health service organizations, or partners and managers in GP practices, should think through their communications priorities and incorporate them in an action plan by which they can monitor and assess progress, using some of the techniques described in the final chapter.

This will help them to develop shared responsibility not only for the ways messages are communicated, and for the success or failure of the process, but for understanding them in the first place.

Executive members of a health authority or trust may be engaged in highly sensitive discussions with hospital consultants, MPs, GPs and the community health council on a strategy to reduce surplus in-patient acute services, develop day surgery, and support new services in the community. The strategy and the discussions could be in tatters overnight if the non-executives have not been involved from the start and, failing to recognize or grasp the issues, are telling local opinion formers on their personal and social circuits that the organization's motives are to cut costs and save money.

A communications action plan concentrates the minds of those who act and speak for the organization. It makes them think about the people who matter, how they will establish or strengthen dialogues with them, and how they will involve them whenever it is appropriate. It helps to ensure wise investment of time, effort and money in communications. It also uses many of the components described in the chapters that follow.

2

Communicating with the 'big three' audience groups

The most important people in any health service are the patients, their families or friends, and other users. Every part of the service is geared to ensuring their satisfaction during the time or times they need it.

Relationships with most of them are not continuous and are formed mainly from the countless personal interactions with health service staff (Chapter 1). In public relations terms 'the planned and sustained effort to establish and maintain goodwill and mutual understanding' (from the definition in the previous chapter) takes place with three main audience groups:

- staff
- key opinion formers
- news media.

They are the principal groups which help to shape patients' and public's expectations, experiences and views of health services.

They are not, of course, mutually exclusive. Staff are opinion formers. So are the media. But defining the groups in this way enables managers to work out how best to communicate with them, using the different approaches and techniques described in this chapter.

It may not always be easy to strike a balance between the competing needs of these groups, but the manager who neglects any one of them does so at peril of damaging relationships with all of them. It is easier to lose a good reputation than to gain one.

Communicating with staff

The huge shifts in organization and culture which have dominated health services in recent years have made communicating with staff more important than ever. As reorganization followed reorganization, more and more managers came to appreciate that change can be managed effectively only if it commands the understanding and support of staff.

There are other reasons for giving top priority to communications with staff. The link between informed staff and good performance is one reason. Another is that each member of staff is, for better or worse, a channel of information and opinion to a much wider audience.

Understanding how to get messages across to staff, and how to listen and respond to staff concerns, is a crucial skill for today's health service manager.

There will be times when managers want, and need, professional advice and support (from, for example, a public relations officer, perhaps working with an organization development specialist), but the responsibility for effective communications rests unambiguously with line managers. Middle managers especially must develop skills if they are to make the transition from exercising control to being a leader. Withholding rather than sharing information as a means of exercising power is no longer appropriate as a modern management style.

MANAGERS WITH ATTITUDE

Most managers are equipped for communication at its most basic. They have legs for walking the job, eyes for observing, ears for listening to staff and a voice with which to respond. What is often missing is the right attitude.

Withholding rather than sharing information as a means of exercising power is no longer appropriate as a modern management style.

A national survey of NHS communications in the early 1990s showed that communicating with staff was a problem for many NHS managers. The 'best' managers were those who took the trouble to listen to staff and respond to what they heard. Instilling the desire to communicate and the confidence to do it properly depends partly on an appropriate corporate culture. If there is no lead from the top and no commitment to open communication, people down the management chain will work to that example.

Communications also depend to some extent on structure. There must be machinery for collective discussion between managers and staff that separates the bargaining and negotiating role from other aspects of internal communication.

In the main, though, creating the right attitude and giving people the necessary confidence require investment of time and money in communication skills training. Not all people are 'natural' communicators, and most will need formal training at several stages of their career. Ideally, every member of staff should be given basic training in verbal and written communication skills. Many staff also need more specialized tuition in other aspects of communication, such as team briefing, media relations, interviews, and presentation.

It is particularly important that clinical staff, especially those in management roles such as clinical directors, receive training in communication skills – in communicating, for example, with junior doctors and other staff throughout the organization.

UNDERSTANDING YOUR AUDIENCES

The first and most obvious point in communication is to define whom you wish to address on a particular subject. It is not enough to view the entire staff of an organization – whether provider, purchaser or regulator – as a single, homogeneous entity. That is the scatter-gun approach. The solution lies in targeting – or audience segmentation. This simply means dividing staff into discrete and manageable groups which consist of people with a common interest in the subject.

Other ways include targeting staff by department, by professional group (often spread across a number of directorates) or by staff grade. At other times there may be geographical areas to address, or instances where the message is aimed at a small segment, such as working mothers with young children.

Once clear about the group or groups with whom you want to communicate, you need to assess the levels of existing knowledge, attitudes and perceptions to discover how the group receives information at present and judge whether those methods are efficient and accurate.

This involves one of the most neglected areas of communication in the NHS: benchmark research (see Chapter 8). Too many 'communications' initiatives fail because they are built on poor foundations. As a result, money is wasted.

Researching staff understanding and perception can be as easy as meeting small groups over an informal lunch or as complex (and correspondingly expensive) as an interview-based survey, using external consultants.

In between lie options for gathering facts, figures and opinions. Some people opt for 'diagonal slices' which take a snapshot through the organization by selecting groups of people from different parts and levels; others may prefer a quantitative questionnaire, open forums, or to make use of an existing communication channel, such as team briefing.

The choice of method will be dictated partly by the size and nature of the target audience, its physical location and the range and complexity of data required, and partly by the financial constraints. In deciding the extent of research, it should be borne in mind that the more reliable the data, the easier it is to plan responses to any problems.

As with any form of opinion sampling, it is sensible to seek expert help with at least some parts of the operation, even if only in designing a questionnaire that will produce useful and statistically valid results. Piloting a draft version with a small group of staff is also advisable, in order to check both its ease of use and the relevance of the results to the questions asked.

DEVELOPING YOUR MESSAGES

Once you have a clear understanding of your audience, you can begin to define more clearly the messages you wish to communicate. These may range from providing essential information to attempting to enhance the reputation of the organization.

In the case of new employees, some basic information needs to be communicated from the start: an adequate background understanding of the organization, the place of the new person in it, and individual duties and objectives. Factual information (who does what and where things are, etc) needs to be given, but the messages to the newcomers should also reflect the wider purpose, aims and values of the organization. They need to enthuse as well as inform so that recruits quickly feel a sense of belonging and loyalty.

The more challenging task, though, is to develop credible messages that will create understanding and support even at times of change for the individual or the department. If a successful organization is one that is in a dynamic state of change and development, it follows that successful internal communication must help to create a climate where change is accepted as a positive opportunity rather than a perpetual sword of Damocles.

Altering perceptions is rarely easy and your message must be thought through clearly if it is to have any chance of being accepted. It needs five other special qualities if it is to succeed:

1   It must be honest and talk about the world as it appears to the audience it is aimed at. Any message perceived as coming from a

management remote from everyday reality will be discounted and its originators discredited. Remember that one person's plan for rational efficiency saving is another person's fear of job cuts.

2   It must address an issue of concern. Some people argue that all information is of value and more must therefore be better. But the fact is that we each operate a filtering system to limit our information intake to a realistic level. So concentrate on the key issues.

3   It must be clear, not least in the language used. The language has to be appropriate to the audience. This is perhaps the area that causes most difficulty for many people, and is where a public relations practitioner can be of particular help.

4   It should be timely, so that people get the message when they need it. Information that arrives too late is worse than useless, for it sends its own signal about the value placed on good communication.

5   It should be consistent. Most people will know of instances where different parts of an organization put across widely differing messages on the same subject, or where managers say one thing but do another. If the messages seem always to be changing, the chances of securing understanding and support are negligible. That is not to say that a message will not evolve over time as understanding or perception alter. If your communications plan is working, the message will need to be updated, but always within a consistent theme or framework.

GETTING THE MESSAGE ACROSS

In the old days, communications solutions tended to fall into a few categories: send a memo, put up a poster, launch a newsletter. Those days have largely gone, and people responsible for staff communications now call on a much wider range of techniques.

There is no off-the-shelf answer to the question of which technique is best. It will vary according to the number of people being addressed, where they are, the speed at which messages must be communicated, whether the message is 'soft' (as, for example, in building reputation) or 'hard' (factual information), and the effectiveness of existing systems.

The rest of this section looks at some of the techniques that can be used, and summarizes points to remember when making a choice. If you are unsure about the best vehicle for your message, seek advice from a public relations practitioner.

Face-to-face communication

This has always been, and remains, the best way of giving information and receiving feedback – provided you have the time and the skills. It can cover anything from personal objective-setting and appraisal sessions to regular departmental meetings. It is best suited to relatively small numbers. If the messages are complex or include reference information, they should be supplemented with a written summary.

Team briefing

This is an extension of face-to-face meetings, but usually with a much more formal structure. Advantages include the fact that a core brief can be rapidly cascaded downwards, that it can be used to present corporate messages in a consistent way, and that it commits managers to regular communication. Drawbacks include the rigidity of the system, difficulty in passing messages back up the management line, the problem of managers who pass on the core brief without interpretation (and in some cases only in written form) and the problem of catering for night staff and part-time staff. It requires a substantial investment in training – and retraining – to work effectively.

Open forums

These are normally used when there is an issue suited to discussion and debate. The most popular format is a brief opening presentation followed by general discussion and questions, with an impartial moderator. They are sometimes coupled with advice surgeries if the matter being discussed has repercussions needing to be dealt with on a one-to-one basis.

Teleconferencing

This is the latest extension of this idea and involves individuals or groups having a sound and video link between different locations.

Normal practice is for all contributions to be routed through the chairman. However, the technology can inhibit many people and the absence of conventional body language signals can affect the dynamics of the meeting.

Staff journals (see also Chapter 6)

Staff journals are still a favourite method of communication. They range from weekly or fortnightly photocopied sheets to monthly or quarterly publications, produced and printed professionally. Many organizations produce more than one type: a simple weekly sheet for conveying managerial and work-related information, and a less frequent but larger, sometimes more upmarket, product that can be used for more general news and features. A drawback is the difficulty of obtaining feedback through journals. They also need a measure of editorial independence. A journal that is regarded as no more than a mouthpiece for senior management will struggle to maintain credibility. Distribution is another area to watch. Too many publications languish unread because the organization fails to deliver them to potential readers.

Notice boards

If attractively presented and positioned well at key locations, notice boards can be useful for conveying information, but they can become mural scrap heaps if they are not properly maintained and kept up-to-date. They need to be in one person's care and sited carefully rather than placed on the nearest piece of blank wall. There should be an agreed period of time for notices to stay up, after which they should be removed. It is even worth insisting on standard sizes and minimum standards of presentation. A 'fast news' notice board, with its own distinct heading and colouring, can be reserved for a copy of the latest staff news bulletin and other topical or urgent information. Again, it is vital that items are displayed and removed promptly.

Audio-visual productions (see also Chapter 6)

These consist mainly of overhead transparencies, videotape, slide-tape and audio tape.

Overhead transparencies are the cheapest form of visual production, but even these should be produced in a professional way. A hand-written overhead, or one covered in acres of small type, may distract the audience and bury your message.

Videotape is a potent method of conveying impressions, although it is less useful for imparting detailed knowledge unless it is part of a structured learning session and accompanied by written notes. Tapes need to be produced to professional standards: everyone is accustomed to broadcast television quality. Videotapes can be expensive to produce, although the involvement of medical illustration departments, film schools and university art faculties can trim production costs dramatically. A video is best used in small groups of six to eight people.

Slide-tape presentations can be used for larger audiences. Again, photography and commentary should be of a high standard. A sophisticated slide-tape show, using multiple projectors and special effects, can be as costly as a video production.

Audio tapes can be produced relatively cheaply, possibly with the help of the facilities and staff at a local radio station. They may offer a useful way of reaching staff spread across a wide area or who do not work in offices. Audio tapes are best used in conjunction with accompanying notes. Another option is to create a 'looped' audio tape of up-to-the-minute news that runs continuously on a dedicated internal telephone extension. A professional commentator should be used, if possible, to bring the contents to life. A second line with an answering machine can be set up so that questions and feedback can be recorded straightaway.

Electronic networks

Computerization provides new opportunities for better internal communication – not just through corporate databases which improve general access to information, but also through the increasing use of networks which link all an organization's computers to a central system. These networks can be programmed to display news items or core team briefs when someone first enters the system; they also require users to confirm they have seen the message or messages before gaining further access to other parts of the system. Central records can indicate how widely the messages have been dispersed, although the system cannot stop people from 'ticking the box' without actually reading or understanding them.

Another drawback of electronic notice boards is the lack of inter-personal contact which helps people to understand and interpret information, and which provides the channel for feeding staff views back along the management line.

Exhibitions and displays (see also Chapter 6)

These can range from permanent displays about a particular service to short-term exhibitions as part of a specific campaign or communications initiative. In either case they need to be displayed to professional standards to catch the eye and impart information. The amount of text should be limited. Photographs should be good. The display should be at a readable height and well lit. It should be sited where people not only pass regularly but can stop without causing congestion.

Annual reports

Annual reports can reinforce key messages and corporate objectives, but all too often they are produced too late to be useful. It is better to produce a report quickly, even if the figures for it are provisional, than to wait for months until every 'i' has been dotted and every 't' crossed. The report should be a means of conveying a sense of achievement and identifying prospects and challenges, rather than a detailed record of budget-balancing. It is also better to avoid producing a glossy report which may look self-indulgent. Produce instead an inexpensive but attractive document that can be distributed to all staff.

Annual general meetings

Annual reports may be used in conjunction with an annual general meeting at which the senior management team reports briefly on the year, answers questions, receives feedback and opens up broad discussion of issues facing the organization.

External media

Newspapers, radio and television play a large part in influencing staff perceptions. Indeed, unless you have a very fast information network, staff may learn things about their organization and their jobs from the local media first. Although it is unwise to rely on external media to keep staff informed (they are, after all, outside your control and will often not cover a subject or will cover it in an unhelpful way), they can be a useful secondary means of communication. Conversely, internal channels should be used to counteract the negative media coverage that every part of the health service receives at some time or another.

Communicating with key opinion formers

If a health service organization is not shaping the opinions of key opinion formers, someone else is – possibly someone with their own, competing agenda.

If the organization is undergoing radical change, opinion formers will be influenced not only by their own and other people's interpretations of what the change is all about, but by existing beliefs about the organization and the way it functions. In such circumstances, an organization is at risk of being trapped between a powerful mythology about the past (days when matron reigned infallibly, clinical mistakes never occurred and waiting lists were non-existent) and sceptical or hostile interpretations of its future.

At worst, failure to build effective relationships with opinion formers can completely undermine an organization's ability to manage. In the public sector, in particular, organizations can find themselves simply reacting to an agenda that is being shaped 'out there' through the various impacts of pressure groups, politicians, professional interests and the news media. Achievement of the organization's objectives then becomes secondary to handling the consequences of attempts by individuals and other organizations to pursue theirs.

Opinion formers matter, and building good relationships with them matters.

WHO ARE OPINION FORMERS?

Opinion formers, both nationally and locally, are not a coherent group. All they have in common is an ability to influence the views of a wide body of people or to influence those who take decisions that affect a wide body of people. The additional weight attached to their views may derive from (with examples in brackets):

- the legitimacy with which they can speak on behalf of a community (MPs and councillors)

- professional status (doctors and lawyers)

- office (committee and association chairmen)

- acknowledged expertise (academics, critics and commentators)

- celebrity status (television and stage personalities)

- influence over the content of newspapers, magazines, radio and television (news, features and commissioning editors, producers and researchers)

- ability to represent a particular group in society or a particular cause (religious and trade union leaders, leaders of charities and pressure groups)

- access to, and understanding of, decision makers (civil servants, personal assistants to top managers, research assistants to MPs, friends and acquaintances).

BUILDING A CASE

No amount of contact-building with opinion formers will do any good if the case that an organization is trying to advance is weak in the first place.

One of the most effective ways to ensure this does not happen is to anticipate the questions, criticisms and fears that are likely to emerge when the case is first exposed to public debate. Good anticipation depends on knowing who are the people likely to be interested in the issue, what their agendas are and what the relationships are likely to be between them.

Building relationships with opinion formers is not, therefore, simply about taking an organization's case and packaging it in a way that makes it attractive to them. Preparation, as described above, can produce fundamental changes in policy formulation and implementation.

MAKING A START

An organization ought to be able to map who the opinion formers are on any issue, what the nature of their interests are, and which relationships between them are of significance or potential significance. This is best done by a small to medium group so that the intelligence that exists inside the organization about opinion formers is fully exploited.

Figure I shows what such a map might look like for a health authority about to undertake a review of acute services. It is very much simplified, but it should stimulate a number of important questions:

- What are the most important relationships for us? And what are the key influences on those relationships?

- What are the other relationships we need to understand?

- If the support of the local MP is crucial to the review, how do we go about achieving that – directly, or through another organization or individual?

- Are our assumptions about GP fundholder hostility to the review safe, or do we need to explore further their opposition?

- Do the public positions of some of the organizations mask important differences within them (between, say, a trust's management and its key doctors, or between councillor and officer views of the important issues)?

- What is the relationship between the timetable for the review and the order in which we tackle opinion formers? What is the relationship between our timetable and important timetables faced by other organizations (for example, local and national election timetables, trust business planning cycles and community care planning cycles)?

- Taking each opinion former in turn, what can we say about their likely reaction to the review? What do we know about the alliances they have, or are planning to develop?

- Who in the health commission is best placed to develop links with the local medical committee chairman, with the medical directors in the acute providers and with the chairman of the council's social services committee?

- If there are gaps in the map, how do we fill them?

By tackling questions suggested by a basic map of relationships, any organization can begin to develop a realistic plan designed to ensure that it maximizes its ability to influence the views of opinion formers.

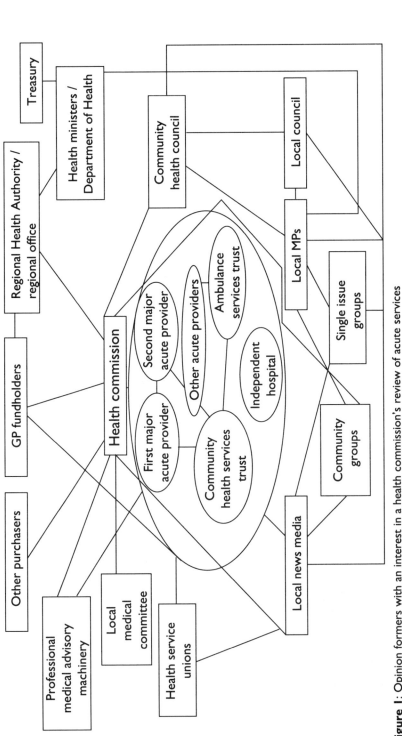

Figure 1: Opinion formers with an interest in a health commission's review of acute services

BUILDING RELATIONSHIPS

Building good relationships with opinion formers requires:

• planning

• imagination

• research

• sharing of information inside the organization.

Planning

Effective relationships with opinion formers take time to develop, demand regular contact and are best established away from the emotional and political heat generated by a crisis.

Too many organizations fail to plan the building of relationships with opinion formers. As a result, when a crisis looms, they lack the standing that is necessary to ensure they are listened to. When they want to do something that carries some risk, they lack the ability to sound out privately one or two key individuals. And when rival interests lobby an opinion former, the latter is unlikely to turn to the affected organization for an alternative briefing.

Good relationships are characterized by ease of contact, honesty (even to the extent of distinguishing between private and public positions on an issue), sharing of intelligence, ability to tap into each other's contacts, and recognition that strains over particular issues do not jeopardize the underlying stability of the relationship.

For any local health service organization, there will be a number of individuals and organizations with whom a steady relationship is important. These include:

• chairmen, non-executives, executives and senior colleagues in other health service organizations

• key hospital consultants and GPs

• local MPs

• key councillors and council officers

• news editors and health reporters on local newspapers and radio stations.

The importance of other organizations and individuals will depend very much on local circumstances and the nature of the issue. A review of maternity services would, for example, automatically bring into play local women's groups, local health visitors' and midwives' associations, and councillors and council committees with a particular interest in women's issues.

Imagination

Apart from inadequate planning, the most common failure in building relationships with opinion formers is lack of imagination. Too many organizations make little or no attempt to put themselves in the shoes of the organization or individual they are trying to influence.

When this happens, opinion formers are sent literature that is of no relevance whatsoever to them, or information that is so detailed, or written from such a narrow professional or managerial point of view, that it is next to useless. The effect is the reverse of what was intended: the organization's standing falls rather than rises and its ability to influence is diminished rather than enhanced.

To avoid this, put to one side what you want to say and focus on how you want each opinion former to respond. Why should they respond in that way? What is in it for them? Do you understand the pressures they are subject to? How can you make the issue more relevant to them? For an MP, for example, you may want to express the issue in terms of impact on his or her constituents.

Research

The imaginative leap into the opinion former's shoes can be supported by some basic research. The more important the opinion former, the more desirable it is to have a detailed picture. In the case of MPs, there are a number of important published sources. Andrew Roth's *Parliamentary Profiles* provides detailed 'warts-and-all' profiles of every MP, and each issue of the House of Commons *House Magazine* carries an interview with an MP about the influences on his or her career.

The political commentators in the quality national newspapers are worth reading for their interpretation of trends in politics and their impact on the political parties. They and lobby correspondents convey a sense of the day-to-day pressures that regulate the lives of national politicians. Look out also for editorials in national and local newspapers, since these will always be read by politicians.

Given the importance of local government and health service relations, local government publications are worth looking at regularly. *Local Government Chronicle* provides comprehensive weekly coverage of local government affairs and provides a useful perspective on where health fits at any time in local government's order of priorities. Local newspaper reporting of local government affairs should also be scanned.

At a local level, existing contacts will provide a means of establishing links with other opinion formers. For example, links at a senior level with a voluntary organization will provide routes into other voluntary organizations, fresh perspectives on community care, a more rounded view of the main 'players' in the local council, and channels into the national 'parents' of key local voluntary organizations.

It is important that contacts are maintained and refreshed since relationships between opinion formers can change rapidly, as can the influence of a particular opinion former. An out-of-date map of opinion formers may be as dangerous as no map at all. Maintaining the map may not be as time-consuming as it sounds. Most organizations will develop a range of important contacts with whom they are in touch on a routine basis and who can routinely update the organization's map of opinion formers. The answer is to get senior managers into the habit of routinely scanning for important external shifts in opinion, policy or relationships.

Sharing information inside the organization

An organization's approach to opinion forming needs to be corporate. No single individual in an organization can develop all the contacts and gather all the intelligence on which to build an organization's entire strategy for influencing opinion formers.

Executive and non-executive directors will have different contacts, and relatively junior staff can often have important contacts in other organizations which are extremely useful when a low-level approach is all that is needed.

Knowledge of these contacts needs to be shared and updated regularly if the organization is to make the most of them. Most managers will know of problems they have faced which could have been solved if they had simply been aware that so-and-so had known so-and-so.

Many trust and authority boards have regular intelligence-sharing sessions which can be used in this way. Functional and line managers should have similar sessions with their own staff which can feed into senior management meetings.

Communicating with the news media

A by-product of the health service reforms in 1990 was a sharper recognition among managers of the connection between news media coverage and public confidence in local health services. They recognized that the persistent drip, drip of critical reporting can not only undermine the morale of staff and the confidence of patients, but can affect the financial success of the business.

At worst, a series of damaging reports about a hospital or community service can result in an exodus of its best staff and pressure on those who remain. That in turn can lead to poor performance, more criticism from users, the public and patients' 'watchdogs' – and more bad publicity.

On the other hand managers who work hard and consistently at spreading the word about their organization's achievements, and who are ready to explain how they are tackling problems and shortcomings when they occur, may find that their staff's pride in the organization and in their job is enhanced by good media coverage, and that patients approach the service in a mood of confidence and co-operation.

Health service managers have to remember that the media do not exist to do them and the health services favours. The manager who has an understanding of media needs and the way they work will be more likely to enlist their co-operation and ensure positive rather than negative or bad publicity. If he or she regularly subjects them to an ear-bashing about their inadequacies (however justified it may seem at the time), the manager and the organization will suffer – and very publicly.

WHAT AND WHO ARE THE NEWS MEDIA?

News, like health care, is a 24-hour business, as anyone knows who has had to give condition checks on babies or celebrities in intensive care units. The media world and its processes are often viewed with bewilderment by health service managers (though their wonder is nothing compared to that of journalists when they look at the Byzantine structure of health service organization).

The news media can be broadly divided into:

* local newspapers

* national newspapers and magazines

* news agencies and freelances

* television and radio.

Local newspapers

These serve areas of towns and villages, or metropolitan districts. Many of them are now free, but, paid for or not, their aims are much the same: to reflect the life of the community and to be commercially viable. Their editors are aware of the partisan views, arbitrary state-ments and sheer emotionalism expressed in much of what they print, but it is their job to report what people do and say without bias and as accurately as possible.

Many health service managers and their staff have good relation-ships with the local press. Regular press conferences or briefings are held by managers, and sometimes by their chairmen, to review items of interest to the community. These meetings are valuable and help to foster friendly relations.

They and the more informal one-to-one meetings between health service managers and the press – as when, for example, they cross paths at local functions – help to give a human face to the management side of the service.

Regrettably, economic pressures on newspapers in recent years have meant that fewer reporters have been available to get out of the office and meet their contacts. Managers should still try wherever possible to establish and cultivate that one-to-one relationship which can make so much difference. Local journalists rightly complain some-times that they are expected to understand the health services, but many health service managers make little attempt to understand the media.

National newspapers and magazines

The national press takes little or no interest in local affairs unless they point up some aspect of a national story; and 'the man on the Clapham omnibus' is not interested in 'the man on the Birmingham omnibus' unless he is a victim when it crashes with loss of lives.

Innovations which have much more than local significance – new approaches to medical treatment, for example – will interest national newspapers. So will changes in services which appear to hit at vulnerable sections of the community, such as children or old people.

The impact of national newspaper reporters, photographers and camera crews covering a story in a normally quiet, unnewsworthy area can be disconcerting, even unnerving, partly because of the siege-like atmosphere that develops and partly because of the speed and pressure at which journalists work, sometimes taking short cuts through back doors and complex issues (not least health service ones) and turning greys into blacks and whites. The speed and ferocity of a media pack in full cry can be daunting.

In the magazine field, specialist journals offer the best chance for managers and other health service staff to reach a particular professional or occupational group through the news, features or letters columns. And many of them are interested in news photographs featuring members of the profession or occupation covered by the journal.

The mass circulation magazines, with their own writers, advisers and regular contributors, are less accessible to occasional contributors, but should not be ruled out as possible vehicles of information in, for example, such things as preventive medicine and health promotion.

News agencies and freelances

News agencies are commercial organizations which provide news as a commodity or a service. They employ their own staff and freelances to supply news and features to newspapers, magazines, radio and television.

The biggest agency in the UK is the Press Association (PA) with its head office in London and reporters based in the main metropolitan cities. The PA maintains a constant flow of news, briefings and features to national and local media. Other, smaller agencies scattered throughout the country feed into the national and local media.

This news-gathering network is completed by hundreds of self-employed freelance journalists, some of whom specialize in certain fields, such as industrial news or health and social affairs – and by staff employed on local newspapers who act, quite legitimately, as correspondents for national newspapers and other media. This often explains why a story given to a local newspaper can appear, very thinly disguised, in major national or regional newspapers or on radio or television.

Television

In news and current affairs programmes, television reports on events and issues in much the same way as the press does, but often with greater impact on people's minds than the printed word. A short item and 'sound bite' in a television programme may convey more than a whole page of newsprint.

Television can work in favour of an organization with a good story to tell and, properly handled, can do more for public relations than any other medium. The BBC and ITV companies are always open to suggestions for programmes, but, like newspapers, they are not servants of the health service manager, who will have no control over the cameras or the editing of the programmes and news items.

Again, like the press, television must always keep the public reaction in mind. The viewer can become easily bored and literally switch off. So while they may be informative, programmes mostly emphasize the human touch and avoid masses of statistics and detail.

Regional television, which provides viewers with a nightly digest of local topics, is constantly on the look-out for material with human appeal, of the kind found in health services. It also likes interesting items that can be expounded by an interviewee who can talk with authority and is, in the widest sense of the word, attractive. An interview gives an opportunity to promote initiatives and inform the public. Its impact is greater than a line in a five-minute news bulletin, however valuable that in itself might be.

Cable television is expanding rapidly, giving increasing scope for coverage of local issues.

Radio

The impact of radio should never be underestimated. It is a media growth area – more than 200 radio stations in the UK, a number which is increasing all the time. Many people still treasure the ability to get on with something else while being entertained and informed.

Although national radio capitalizes on the appeal of health topics and issues, it is in local radio that the best and most accessible opportunities lie. Local radio stations are demonstrably conscious of their community roles and are keen to report and discuss local health issues. Their interest is not confined to news bulletins. Health news and information can be introduced into a wide variety of programmes, ranging from regular broadcasts on health affairs through specialist programmes for people with disabilities to the ubiquitous 'phone-in'.

GATHERING THE NEWS

Most of the time, health service managers are dealing with local journalists who get their stories from four main sources:

1 'diary' dates, such as council meetings, courts, and other public events

2 routine check calls to emergency services, hospitals, and other 'contacts' with whom journalists talk regularly

3 people who get in touch with them

4 other news media.

Managers should be able to anticipate most of the media enquiries in the first two categories. The other two sources are less predictable.

People who contact the media often do so because they have a grievance. They have felt let down or badly treated by a service; or they want, for perhaps personal or political reasons, to cause embarrassment to an organization or a public figure. They are much less likely to contact the media if a service is reliable and satisfactory. Good service is what they pay for (albeit indirectly in the case of the NHS) and is what they feel entitled to expect.

Only an irresponsible manager ignores repeated complaints or blames them on the media. More likely they will point to weaknesses or failures that need attention. They must be investigated, if only in the end to restore public confidence.

If all the media receive, and report on, are complaints, the public will get a lop-sided view of the service. However uphill the task may seem at first, the manager has to make a conscious and continuing effort to tell journalists about health service achievements – provided the achievements are human ones and not simply to do with statistical progress, which can often be fragile, short-lived and open to various interpretations. The health service trust which presents good performance as merely recovery from financial deficit, rather than tangibly better services for patients, is in for a bad press.

No public relations, however skillful, can disguise a poor product, but successful media relationships can make sure that users' perceptions of services are not soured by bad coverage before they walk through the door.

The fourth major source of stories is other media. Newspapers, news agencies, magazines, radio and television feed off each other. Editors and news editors planning what stories should be covered each day will have before them all the reports their rivals have been publishing and broadcasting during the previous 12 to 24 hours. Local newspapers look at the national press to see if there is a 'local angle' to major national stories. National media receive a constant stream of reports from local media and from local freelance journalists. Correspondents from overseas media scan local and national reports for things that will be of interest to their readers in their home countries.

From all these sources will emerge the 'brief' that a news desk (the centre of the news-gathering operation) allocates to the reporters. If the brief is based on what someone has told them in, say, an angry telephone call, or on the way the story has been presented in the national media, it can be difficult for a local manager to shake that perception, however distorted it might be. And news editors are not at all keen to have their reporters spending half a day on a story that turns out to be not as interesting as it seemed.

THREE GOLDEN RULES

There are three golden rules to media relationships:

Rule 1: Be active. Do not wait for stories to come to you. Think of the stories you can present which record your success. And do it in ways that will appeal to the media you are aiming at.

Rule 2: Be first. Once a story has 'broken', and particularly if it is a nasty one, it could be halfway round the world let alone the town before you have a chance to put your perspective on it. Explaining that 'it isn't quite like that' when the story is up and running is a very hard task. People have already grasped the essential points, formed a view, and may not even see or hear subsequent denials or qualifications.

Rule 3: Plan ahead. The only way you can hope to have a clear run with your news or announcement is to plan, and think about:

- timing, in relation to media deadlines
- the setting for your announcement, looking at whether you want to be at the location involved or in your office or board room
- the participants – the people who you want to take the lead
- what else is going on, so that you are not upstaged by another, 'competing' event.

A 'good story'

Journalists like to argue that there is a faculty called 'news sense' which media people have and other mortals lack. It is true that an instinctive feeling about a story often makes an editor splash it on page one or hide it on page nine, but there are some clues which can help a health service manager to recognize what journalists are interested in.

Good stories are often those which create an emotional response, or that a lot of people can share in, because they relate to a common experience.

Stories which prompt joy, fear, excitement, pity or outrage clearly make 'strong' copy. So do stories which affect a large number of people – if only to tell them that their rates are going up or that their hospital may close.

continued

A 'good story' (continued)

The media also have a special relish for anything which makes a public authority look an ass. They love the million-pound gas bill, the hole in the newly-surfaced road and the wrong kind of snow.

They have their own vocabulary which turns every disagreement into a row, every refusal into a snub, every investigation into a probe and every confidence into a secret, and they have their own headline language such as: 'Fury over "bubbly" for private patients' or 'Watchdog raps health chief'.

What brings all these ingredients together more often than not are people. Stories about organizations and policies have their place, but the best stories have 'human interest' as the main ingredient.

Individual babies, children, mothers, grannies, nurses, surgeons, midwives, therapists, paramedics can illustrate the qualities and achievements of a service – and its shortcomings – much more effectively than statistics and strategies.

COMMUNICATING WITH THE MEDIA – THE METHODS

The press release

This is a highly effective means of communicating consistent messages to large numbers of media. Some journalists say press releases go straight in the bin. Many do. But many do not, particularly if they are properly aimed at the target newspaper, magazine or radio or television station. A press release has to be relevant to the media you send it to. Nothing irks journalists more than ill-directed press releases sent out by a scatter-gun approach to as many media as can be found in a directory.

But if they are written well and targeted carefully, press releases remain the best way to reach the most people for the least expense. They allow you to say what you want to say rather than something you wish you had not. They are authoritative and they help to ensure not only consistency in the messages you are giving to the media, but consistency in the messages you are giving to other groups, such as staff or local authorities. And, of course, they can be used for reference afterwards.

Press releases need to be written from the top down – see Figure 2. For managers accustomed to writing documents with an introduction, a weighing-up of arguments and a conclusion, this is a new lesson to learn. The same principles apply for press release writers as for journalists: if you have not grabbed the reader's attention in the first sentence you have almost certainly failed.

Writing a press release is an exercise in clarifying a message, ranking the points you want to make in priority order and then presenting them in the kind of language you might use to tell the story to friends or family.

It should also be possible to cut the story from the bottom upwards, so that if all that survives is the first paragraph, it encapsulates the essentials of the story.

As a general rule it is best to avoid trying to say too much, and to cover three or four main points. Then support these with facts and spice them with quoted remarks. Journalists want facts: How much did it cost? How many people work there? How many patients will it treat? If you do not supply them the journalists will obtain them elsewhere.

Sending out a press release without quotes invites the reporter to telephone you – possibly when it is inconvenient – for a few hasty remarks, or to make up a quote based on contents. It is much better to have thought out what you you want to say and to get it in the press release first.

The release should be produced in one-and-a-half or double line spacing and on one side of the paper only. It should be sent by fax or first-class post, or delivered by hand.

Every health organization should have an accurate and up-to-date list of the telephone and fax numbers and addresses of their media contacts. An associated list should give the names, addresses and fax numbers of people who should also receive the press release for information, such as non-executive members of the board, the community health council and MPs.

The telephone interview

The press release may be all that is needed to communicate a message to the media, but it is also an invitation to do business – the start of a dialogue with the journalists. The next stage may be the telephone interview, far and away the most common method used by journalists to obtain their information.

RAILTON HEALTHCARE TRUST[1]

Bridge Park, Railton, Bromshire RL12 8RN
Telephone 01234 567890 Fax 01234 987654[2]

PRESS RELEASE   4 January 1995[3]

OLYMPIC STAR TO OPEN COUNTY'S FIRST POLYCLINIC[4]

Railton's £3 million polyclinic, the first in Bromshire, will be officially opened by Olympic gold hurdler Peta Davies on Wednesday 18 January 1995 at 2.30 pm.[5]

Peta, daughter of one of the GPs based at the polyclinic, Dr Eric Davies, will unveil a plaque in the reception area.

Railton Healthcare Trust has set the pace in developing new services in the community, with the purpose-built polyclinic – Honeymeads – as the focus for them. Consultants ←6
from Railton General Hospital are now holding out-patient medical and surgical clinics there. Physiotherapists and speech therapists have also transferred some of their work to Honeymeads.

Two local GP practices have moved into the building, which also includes a minor surgery unit, X-ray department, pharmacy, chiropody unit and multi-purpose rooms for child health clinics and for people to see their health visitor, district nurse, or community psychiatric nurse.

The polyclinic opened its doors three months ago. Trust chief executive Tom Gordon said today: "It has brought many NHS services under one roof and made them much more accessible. Patients and other people who use it already regard it as an outstanding success.

"The official opening will give us a chance to say a big thank-you to everyone who worked so hard to ensure its success."

– ends –

For more information, please contact Tom Gordon, chief executive, or Dr Ann Bailey, medical director, at the Trust's offices (address and telephone number above).[7]

Figure 2: A press release with: [1]The name of the organization issuing the release. [2]The full address and telephone and fax numbers. [3]Date of the release. [4]Heading indicating the contents. [5]An opening paragraph giving the main points of the release, followed by the key facts. [6]Double or one-and-a-half line spacing. [7]The name of the sender and/or other contact.

In that or any other circumstances the call can seem very urgent and important. The pace of news-gathering is hectic as one deadline piles on another – continuous or hourly news programmes on radio and news agencies feeding an omnivorous media. But try not to be intimidated and resist the temptation to make off-the-cuff responses. You want to try to avoid a situation where you forget to make a particular point or wish you had said something differently, or of course, not said anything at all.

Try not to be intimidated.

Ask the journalist how much time there is, and use some of it to think through what you want to say and how you want to say it. Do not delay unnecessarily, but do not be panicked either. And, of course, if it is your press release which has prompted the questions, you should have the answers ready.

It is legitimate for journalists to take notes of your conversation from the moment it starts. They do not have to announce, 'I am writing this down'. You should assume that they are writing it down and that everything is on the record (see page 42). He or she may also be recording the conversation on audio tape. Assume that this is the case, and then you will not be in for any surprises.

Radio reporters will almost invariably tell you when a tape recorded interview starts, and you should make sure you know when it is finished. Best of all, be clear about what you want to say before the conversation gets underway; and do not say anything you would not want published or broadcast.

The television or radio interview

Before accepting or declining an invitation to give a television interview, it is worth weighing up the advantages and disadvantages of appearing. There are few occasions that bring no benefits to a health service organization or manager, not least because an interview can give lie to the image of the 'faceless bureaucrat'. However, it is worth bearing in mind that a doctor has instant credibility, and a clinical director, public health doctor or GP may win supporters and influence people more successfully than a non-clinical manager.

This has to be balanced against the desirability of destroying the image of 'faceless bureaucrats'. Chairmen, non-executives and executives should use every media opportunity to put their messages across (provided they are united about them). If any of them are intimidated by the medium they can receive training, preferably given by experienced television and radio broadcasters. The training is not designed to produce instant media stars, but does impart the tricks of the trade and helps create self-confidence.

The most important trick of all for the interviewee is preparation and deciding in advance the points that need to be made. This is more vital today, in the era of the 'sound-bite', than it has ever been. It is amazing to find people who will spend hours preparing a talk to the local Soroptomist or Rotary Club giving only passing thought to what they are going to say to the many thousands of people watching television or listening to the radio.

The difference between a live and a recorded interview should also be remembered. Only in the former will the interviewee be sure that what he or she is saying is actually being heard. Recorded items will almost certainly be edited. The interviewee can advise on the relative importance of the various statements he or she has made, but has no control over what is transmitted.

Managers who are keen to appear on television should not complain at what they regard as lack of interest by the local television station. They should make a point of contacting the station and telling the news editor of a particular issue they think should be aired. The main thing is to take the initiative, to think positively and not to let opportunities slip by.

Much the same applies to radio – in fact, more so. With its strong involvement in the affairs of a defined community, local radio is a particularly valuable medium. Its news bulletins report and reflect a wide variety of issues and its current affairs programmes are excellent vehicles for longer interviews or discussions.

Many years ago, a BBC training guide described a radio interview as 'a conversation with an aim', in which the 'interviewer is acting on behalf of the well-informed enquiring listener' and takes an approach of 'informed naïvety'. The definition remains an admirable one.

Press conferences

These are best used when you have something formal to say, such as the launch of a major development plan. They can also be a practical and effective measure in, say, a crisis attracting media interest. They bring all the media together at one time and save you having to repeat the same information many times over to individual journalists. They should be held only when there is something worth saying.

If you have time to plan, make sure that all the journalists start from the same baseline. Give each one a summary or press release containing the main points of what you are going to say and including the names and titles of the people giving the press conference. Do not assume the journalists have come with background knowledge.

Be ready to make your three or four main points, and think in advance how you might express them crisply in a phrase or sentence that sums up your messages. Ask yourself the questions you hope you won't get asked about contentious issues or crises. In that way, you will be ready for the worst.

Allow time for individual interviews by radio and television reporters as soon as the main press conference is over.

When it's your turn on TV or radio...

If you are to be interviewed on television or radio, you should be concise and committed, know what you want to say and make sure you say it – even if the interviewer does not ask the 'right questions'. People may explain away missed opportunities by saying, 'The interviewer didn't ask me', but no politician has yet said that.

Whether on television or radio bear in mind that you almost certainly know more about the subject than the interviewer. You should:

- say what needs to be said clearly and concisely, without padding

- talk positively in a conversational tone, using everyday language people can easily understand

- avoid jargon or abbreviations, such as 'fundholders', 'internal market' or 'FHSA'

- give information in a simple form and without reading from notes (but have a note of key facts and figures on a piece of paper that can be referred to if necessary)

- aim to get across two or three points, not nine or ten

- avoid writing a script and rehearsing lines

- be prepared for questions that you hope will not be asked.

If going on television, you should:

- sit comfortably and reasonably upright. A 'laid-back' style, with feet outstretched and arms dangling, may be cool, but it can also look close to arrogance

- look at the interviewer, not at the camera

- keep going, even if the interview seems to be turning out badly and missing important points. The interview will not look as bad to the viewer as it may feel to you.

'Off the record' and 'non-attributable' information

In a relationship of mutual trust, a health service manager and a journalist will be able to talk to each other off the record as well as on the record. A prepared press statement is on the record. So is anything said by the manager which he or she decides can be quoted word-for-word for publication and can be attributed to him by name. The manager should think before speaking and choose words carefully.

There may be times (though it is wise to keep them as few as possible) when the manager prefers to go 'off the record' – that is, to say something or give information which is strictly not for publication. There are two main reasons for going off the record:

1   The information which has been supplied on the record gives an incomplete or misleading account and will prevent the journalist from writing a balanced story. Off-the-record information is in no way attributable to the source, but enables the journalist to gain a full understanding of the issue.

2   The story into which a journalist is enquiring may be personally or politically sensitive. The manager may wish to explain off the record why he or she is being awkward or less than co-operative and putting the relationship with the journalist under strain. If they have a good understanding, the journalist may agree to postpone or even, in extreme cases, quash the story once he or she is put in the picture and accepts the wisdom of doing so. Journalists will not, however, fly in the face of what they reasonably consider to be the public interest.

Sometimes the manager and the journalist will agree, after discussing an issue off the record, that an on-the-record comment of some sort can be made. The manager must state clearly to the journalist that he or she wishes to go off the record before anything is said, and secure an agreement to honour the request. A breach of the agreement would be a breach of trust.

But in dealing with journalists he or she does not know, the manager should stay on the record. Most of the journalists would not see the manager as a valuable contact and may have few qualms about quoting off-the-record information.

Alternatively comments or explanations can be offered to journalists as non-attributable which means they can use them for background but not linked to the informant.

If you are a press officer or manager with responsibility for press relations, you should:

- be completely trusted, with access at all times to the chief executive and chairman, able to see any papers and be briefed on every contentious issue. In a hospital, you must have access to all clinical directors, non-clinical directors and senior nursing staff. Most likely, you will quickly become part of the 'fabric', known and trusted by ward staff and medical and scientific staff – all the people who could be the subject of media interest at any time.

- have secure information sources. If you do not know the answer, you must be able to find the person who does – quickly – and must keep a contacts book at home for after-hours calls.

- be accessible to the media. Journalists who telephone the workplace must be able to get the press officer, public relations officer or deputy.

- understand the process. A minor local story can become a tabloid splash in no time and then develop all sorts of unforeseen angles. Anticipate not only the questions, but also where the story may go from there.

- use your position in the organization to cross-examine senior managers and consultants until you are satisfied that comments being made to the public, through the media, are accurate. An organization's reputation can be badly damaged by public statements that are quickly overtaken by events or demolished by journalists' endeavours. Always resist the temptation to add cover-up to cock-up.

- respond at speed and with economy. A newspaper, television or radio deadline is real, and the story will run without a balancing comment that fails to reach the journalist in time. Tomorrow is always too late.

continued

continued

- use words sparingly. Words are precious to a newspaper, particularly to a popular national tabloid, which will never print a 500-word response. The reader is the audience, and the reader has a limited attention span. Use plain English, the language of ordinary people, not the committee room.

- use the letters page if necessary to expand understanding. This page, especially in local newspapers, is well read. If a comment has been ignored, or rejected, get a letter off at once, preferably by fax, for the next edition. Do not attack the editorial integrity of the newspaper (such letters tend not to be published), but briefly make the point that needs to be got over.

- understand radio and television. Local radio is an excellent training ground for managers, clinicians and experts of all kinds. Offer your local station health promotion slots or interviews with the director of public health about local disease prevalence. Television is also useful. Train colleagues to understand television and to be interviewed – the companies will appreciate a professional approach and a more effective message will go out to the audience. Television is about moving pictures as well as talking heads. Consider what footage might be useful to go behind the voice-over – there is no harm in directing the crew to the upgraded ward, for example.

REACTING TO CLINICAL MISTAKES

However careful doctors, nurses and other staff may be, and whatever procedures and safeguards may exist, human error can and will occur from time to time. To maintain public confidence in health services and their staff, it is essential that the media should be given the fullest possible explanation when mistakes happen.

The most sensational stories are likely to appear when the media suspect that information is being deliberately withheld. Given an explanation and reliable information, the media and the public will usually view the mistake, and judge it, with a sense of reason and proper perspective.

When a mistake has obviously occurred – removal of a wrong limb, for example, or an anaesthetic accident leading to brain damage or death – certain broad rules should be followed when dealing with the media:

- Patient confidentiality must be preserved and the name and address of the person involved should not be given without the specific consent or request of the patient or relatives.

- Only basic factual information should be given. Any formal inquiry into the circumstances, which may have to be held later, must not be prejudiced by inaccurate or speculative remarks.

- It should be made clear that the matter is being fully investigated and that any necessary action is being taken to prevent it happening again.

- The apologies – or, if more appropriate, the sympathy – of the organization for those affected should be conveyed.

- Suggestion of bureaucratic 'cover-up' should be avoided.

3

Patients and the media

Most health service managers have at some time or another to confront the need to balance the interests of patients against those of the public and the media.

The demands of journalists after a major incident (a terrorist attack or train crash, for example) or the admission to hospital of a celebrity have to be met. The same applies during an infectious disease outbreak. Neither the demands nor the journalists will go away. Recognition of that simple fact, together with detailed planning, contingency arrangements and good management on the day (or night) will save a lot of hassle and conflict.

This chapter examines many of the media-handling problems and the issues of patient confidentiality.

Major incidents

How health service managers and other professionals, including doctors, respond to the news media in an emergency or crisis will depend partly on the scale and nature of what has happened.

Major incidents normally involve large numbers of casualties. But sometimes an incident involving only a small number of people, or even just one person, may attract as large a number of reporters, television crews and photographers as a major incident. Examples would be the illness or injury of a celebrity or leading politician, or someone undergoing a 'first-ever' operation or medical procedure.

In some instances – after, say, a terrorist attack or a multiple road crash – the police will play a key part in dealing not only with relatives and the public, but with the media, particularly in the first 24 hours or so. On other occasions, health service managers will be in the front line – when, for example, a clinical mistake may have put a life in danger.

Hospitals designated to take casualties after a major incident have introduced procedures largely based on the advice in a health circular, HC(77)1. These procedures are reviewed and tested regularly, sometimes in the light of experience. They include the arrangements for providing information to relatives and friends and the media.

At least one manager, preferably working with the hospital's public relations adviser, should be assigned to deal with the media. This is not only in the interests of journalists but to ensure that the rest of the hospital team are not distracted from their work. The manager and public relations adviser should make themselves known to reporters and establish an early dialogue with them to develop a relationship of mutual help and trust – one in which the hospital and the media recognize the needs and problems of each other.

Journalists must be kept fully informed about the availability of statements and bulletins and told when facilities will be arranged for interviews and pictures. If they are left in the dark about the arrangements or the timing of information, or suspect they are being unreasonably obstructed from doing their job, they will make their own unofficial arrangements.

Handling the media after a major incident can be divided into four main time phases, from the moment the first casualties begin to arrive:

Phase one – the first three or four hours
Phase two – the remainder of the first 24 hours
Phase three – the following 36 hours
Phase four – the recovery period.

PHASE ONE – THE FIRST THREE OR FOUR HOURS

On being informed to expect heavy casualties, the hospital's duty manager should:

• contact the hospital's public relations adviser or press officer (although this may not be necessary if they are called out automatically as part of the major incident procedure)

• get to know the senior uniformed police officer assigned to make the hospital secure and the officer in charge of any specialist unit, such as an anti-terrorist squad.

A liaison officer may be sent to the hospital by police headquarters to co-ordinate the activities of police at the hospital. The liaison officer will have direct contact with his headquarters, with the highest ranking police officer available in the area, and with the casualty bureau switchboard or police press officer, who will deal with calls from relatives. The police will probably stop everybody except essential personnel from entering the hospital at first. Security will be especially tight if there has been a terrorist attack or if police officers have been injured.

Initial interest from the media may come as the accident and emergency department is put on 'red alert' and before the public relations adviser has arrived. The manager may have to speak to these early enquirers and give live radio and television interviews by telephone. In a built-up area, a major incident will snarl up traffic and make it difficult for staff to get in.

Journalists (who may start arriving as soon as the ambulances) will be kept outside the hospital for the time being, but should be allowed in as soon as the police agree. A press room, preferably equipped with telephones, should be set up as near as possible to the accident and emergency department and hospital reception area.

A media briefing should be arranged as soon as possible. The following information should be collected for use in a statement to be issued at the briefing.

- The time the hospital was alerted.

- The number of injured received by the hospital (males, females, children, with their ages).

- The injuries, if only in general terms at first.

- A summary of the treatment being given, including the number of patients being operated on and the number receiving minor treatment.

No personal details about the patients should be issued until confirmation is given by the police that the next-of-kin have been informed. Any information that is given should, if possible, be exactly the same as that provided by the police. The police liaison officer or police press officer may wish to check the statement and to attend the briefing, particularly if police personnel are among the injured.

The statement should be read to journalists and the facts repeated in radio and television interviews. The hospital manager involved may wish to do this but if not, the public relations adviser or press officer should do it. An undertaking should be given that a further statement will be made once further information is known.

It is good practice to announce at this stage that there will be a regular briefing in the press room every hour. That gives journalists confidence in the organization and a point of reference, even if the information does not become available that frequently.

There will be pressure from television crews for 'actuality shots' showing the accident and emergency team in action. This, along with any early interview with a victim(s), might be allowable in some hospitals with experienced doctors and nurses. If it can be done, only one television camera and one stills photographer should be allowed in on a 'pooled' agreement wherein they undertake to share their pictures with other stations and newspapers.

If possible, a senior doctor – the accident and emergency consultant, for example – should be available for interviews during phase one to meet the needs of journalists for updated coverage. This is particularly important if no staff or patients have been available. If there are several television crews, it may be best to arrange for the interviews to take place outside the hospital to avoid a crush inside.

PHASE TWO – THE REMAINDER OF THE FIRST 24 HOURS

Information given in the first media briefing should be confirmed and any telephone calls from the media (for example, local newspapers and radio and television stations asking for details about patients from their areas) should be dealt with. Casualty figures should be double-checked, preferably against the list the hospital has compiled. Any discrepancy from early, and probably accidental, mis-reporting can be put right at this stage.

Fuller information about the injuries and treatment should become available and, again, should be given by a doctor to the media.

Follow-up statements should give:

- the total number of admissions

- the number of deaths

- names of patients (as soon as names are released by the police)

- emergency operations performed

- intensive care cases

- the number of patients.

Times of deaths should be given, together with any information illustrating the efforts that have gone into fighting for the lives of the victims. Journalists will be particularly interested in the younger patients, and even more so if they are small children.

If further developments are likely, briefings should be arranged before 11 am, 5 pm or 8 pm to meet television and newspaper deadlines.

Journalists should be told that there will be no more updates until the next morning. If they know they are being given all reasonable co-operation and are promised a briefing the next day, they will leave. The night duty manager should, however, have a prepared statement to refer to for any enquiries.

If there is a situation in which the media will need constant updates, as when children are fighting for their lives in the intensive care unit, arrangements should be made for overnight and early morning condition checks to be available. Calls may come as late as 2 am and as early as 5 am.

PHASE THREE – THE FOLLOWING 36 HOURS

Journalists will want to interview casualties. They should be allowed to do so unless the doctors, police or the patients themselves object for medical, security or personal reasons. To minimize disruption, a 'press hour' should be arranged when reporters, photographers and television crews are allowed to meet the patients.

In hospitals with experience in major incidents, victims are normally grouped together in the same ward(s) to enable them to share the recovery and overcome the shock of the incident.

Patients prepared to talk to the journalists should, if possible, be grouped together in one part of the ward. The staff should also be asked if they would be willing to talk about how they have coped with the pressure of the emergency and how they have cared for the patients.

If possible, the 'stills' photographers should go in first. A large group of ten or more should be split into two, and each group should be allowed at least five minutes to take their pictures and for their reporters to do their interviews. Radio reporters may also go in at this time for their interviews.

If the patients are feeling tired or distressed by all the questioning and flash bulbs, the television teams may agree to send in only one crew for a single interview and pool the resulting film. Alternatively, they may take in two camera crews and share the reporter. It is a situation often best managed by a public relations person with media-handling experience.

After this 'press hour', the media should not be given further access to the patients unless a patient or the patient's family insist that they want to see a particular journalist, or unless a member of the Royal Family or other distinguished person makes an official visit.

Even in the case of an official visitor, nothing should be arranged that could disrupt the work of the ward and interfere with the recovery of patients. Any media involvement will be dealt with by the visitor's private office and may be restricted to one photographer being allowed to take pictures for subsequent 'pooling'.

PHASE FOUR – THE RECOVERY PERIOD

The intensity of interest will begin to fade during the following days. Any continuing interest will be in condition checks on patients and updates on the more seriously ill people in intensive care. If one of the patients has caught the public's attention, interest might come in the form of national newspapers bringing in sports or entertainment celebrities to be pictured with the patients.

There may be problems caused by 'buy-ups'. This is where a patient's family enters into a financial contract with one newspaper. In such cases, it is best to announce the deal to the rest of the media. They will grumble but understand (since some, given the chance, would have made the same deal). It is important to remember, however, that such 'buy-ups' are between the family and the newspaper and do not bind the hospital or its staff to take part in pictures or interviews, or to give special co-operation to the newspaper concerned.

Patient confidentiality

Illness is a private matter, and confidentiality between doctor and patient must be safeguarded. But managers and public relations people often have to walk a difficult tightrope between the interests of the patient and the interests of the public, particularly when the media are taking an interest in a hospital patient or in the victims of an outbreak of infectious disease.

For 36 years, a circular from the Ministry of Health, HM(56)58, set the official rules as far as patients in hospital were concerned. New draft guidance, covering the whole question of *Confidentiality, Use and Disclosure of Personal Health Information*, has been issued by the Department of Health. It was the subject of formal consultation as *Health Service Public Relations* was going to press.

The draft guidance was based on the principle that information about the health and welfare of a patient:

- 'is confidential to that patient and to those providing the patient with care and treatment

- 'should only be disclosed to those who need to have it in order to provide, plan and manage effective care and treatment

- 'should not be disclosed to other persons without the consent of the patient, except in certain circumstances outlined in the guidance'.

THE DRAFT GUIDANCE

The Department of Health's draft guidance on information to the media about individual patients said NHS bodies should be open with the media and should respond positively to enquiries. They should ensure that a sufficiently experienced and responsible officer is available at all times, whether in person or by telephone, to answer enquiries from the media.

The draft continued:

- The NHS must not, however, disclose personal information to the media (or any other unauthorized person) without the patient's consent, except in the most exceptional of circumstances.

- If approached by a third party (including representatives of the media or anyone thought to be contributing information to the media), neither NHS bodies nor anyone who works in the NHS should confirm that any individual is a patient, or divulge any information about his or her condition, without the patient's consent.

- Subject to the patient's consent, a brief indication of progress may be given in response to a media enquiry, in terms authorized by the health professional principally concerned with the patient's care and treatment (usually the hospital consultant or GP).

- Where the patient is unable to give consent because of incapacity, is a young person unable to consent, or has died, disclosure should be subject to the agreement of the patient's nearest relative(s) or friends.

- Where a patient or ex-patient has invited the media to cover his treatment, the NHS body may comment in public, but should restrict itself to factual information and the correction of incorrect assertion or published comment. In doing so, it must comply with the duty of confidence towards the patient. In cases of doubt, legal advice should be sought.

The draft said there must be a strong public interest in disclosure before the duty of confidence owed to patients could be overridden. Disclosure to a third party of personal health information might, however, still be justified in the public interest. The main justifications are:

- for public accountability and monitoring purposes (for example, publication of NHS statistics)

- serious risk to the health of other individuals

- serious risk to public health

- the reporting of adverse drug reactions

— the prevention, detection or prosecution of serious crime

— disclosures to the professional regulatory bodies, such as the General Medical Council, General Dental Council or United Kingdom Central Council for Nursing, Midwifery and Health Visiting (for example, for the investigation of serious professional misconduct)

— bona fide and approved clinical and scientific research and surveys.

The draft emphasized that the list of possible justifications was not exhaustive, and each request for disclosure of health information must be considered on its merits.

It stated that, following consultation with the appropriate health professional principally responsible for the patient's care and treatment, the disclosure of personal health information might be justified in order to prevent serious harm to the health of another individual. Examples included the reporting of adverse drug reactions and investigation and control of communicable disease.

Health authorities have a general statutory responsibility, and local authorities have specific statutory responsibilities, with regard to communicable disease. By law, certain diseases are subject to specific control measures. A doctor who diagnoses or suspects such a case has to inform the 'proper officer' of the relevant local authority (usually the consultant for communicable disease control) who has wide-ranging powers to prevent the spread of the disease. Disclosure of information by the 'proper officer' in the exercise of those powers can be justified.

For the manager or press officer walking the patient interest-public interest tightrope, the draft guidance is clear but still leaves room for commonsense judgment: 'Disclosure of health information must be considered on its merits'. (See above.)

PATIENTS IN HOSPITAL

A hospital manager or press officer confronted with the media's interest in a particular hospital patient has to observe the guidance but also has to get to grips with the situation. This involves seeing the story not only from the perspectives of the patient, relatives and hospital, but also from those of the media.

That means:

- assessing the news value of the story
- deciding what the pressure will be for photographs, words and film, and in what order
- working out a strategy for handling the media
- acting fast – or being swiftly overtaken by events.

It is possible that hospital staff, under pressure from journalists on the scene, have already provided information they were not authorized to give, such as the location of the ward; or, worse, may have lied to the media: 'No, he's not in this hospital'.

Journalists, like most people doing their job, do not like being lied to. Nor do they like being misled. For example, smuggling patients or relatives out through a side door when the journalists are waiting in reception can cause frustration and anger that they – the manager or press officer – could do without. If asked to do this for the sake of the family, the manager or press officer should admit it to the media once the person they are interested in has gone, and explain that the patient and the family did not want to be interviewed.

Smuggling patients or relatives out through a side door when the journalists are waiting in reception can cause frustration and anger.

Getting close to the patient

From the start, the best approach for the manager or press officer is to:

- get as close as possible to the patient, relatives or friends, and to the consultant in charge of the case

- emphasize to them that journalists will get their information somehow or another, and that it may be from other less reliable sources

- explain to the patient, family or friends that with their help the media interest will be controllable. Regular briefings to the journalists will give them an idea of progress and sufficient news to meet the demands of a continuing story

- point out that the media will not stop reporting about the patient just because the hospital is unco-operative and (again) that, in the absence of help, they will seek their information elsewhere.

If the patient, family and friends see the advantages of one person – the press officer, say – dealing with the media, journalists will go to that person as a source. The press officer will know the deadlines for the daily newspapers and radio and television, and will check the patient's condition at pre-arranged intervals with the nurse in charge without bothering the family.

In the case of famous patients, there will be pressure from the media to interview other people concerned – for example, members of the surgical or medical team and relatives or friends who are relieved now that the danger is past. The press officer can predict demands of these kinds and talk them through beforehand with the patient and the professional staff concerned.

Media arrangements

A press conference, for television and radio as well as national and local press, might be appropriate. The local media should not be overlooked. They get aggrieved to see 'splash' stories in the national press about a well-known patient whose progress they may have followed in a restrained way over several weeks. Ignoring or overlooking them may squander much of the goodwill that may be needed on other occasions.

If a patient who has been the subject of national media interest has a dramatic change of condition for the worse or the better, the press officer should use the Press Association (PA) news agency to put the message out – after clearing the text first with the relatives or patient. The name of the press officer and a deputy should be given as contacts for follow-up calls.

If photographers are waiting for one chance of the first picture of the recovering patient, and if the patient and family or friends are happy, a 'pooled' picture might be organized, preferably through the Press Association, so that it is available in black and white and colour to all media. If the patient is content and fit to be photographed, it is better not to wait until the next day: photographers may try in the meantime to snatch a picture or smuggle in a 'friend' with a camera. Tight control of the situation depends on providing the media with what they want, when they want it, as much as possible.

If the recovery is rapid and sustained, arrangements might be made for pictures of the patient and bedside interviews. There will almost certainly be demands for them. Excessive demand for interviews can be controlled, again by 'pooling' – explaining to the media that the patient is not well enough to meet more than, say, one newspaper reporter, one photographer, one television crew and one radio reporter. That adds up to separate interviews, with 'stills' shots taken while the newspaper reporter is asking the questions.

The media may not like 'pooling' arrangements and may try to resist them. But they will quickly accept them once they see the alternatives are a complete blank. It is up to them to decide who does what. The print journalists will select the reporter, the television organizations will select the crew, and so on. This is a good way of reassuring medical and nursing staff who have seen the huge array of journalists outside and fear for the patient's well-being.

A patient who has fully recovered can, of course, be interviewed by a number of journalists, particularly if leaving hospital. The best thing then is to set up a press conference for all-comers, but keep the time limited to, perhaps, half an hour.

Media conduct

A code of practice drawn up by newspapers and magazines themselves and adopted by the Press Complaints Commission (see Chapter 4) says:

'Journalists or photographers making enquiries at hospitals or similar institutions should identify themselves to a responsible executive and obtain permission before entering non-public areas.'

It adds that the restrictions in the code on intruding into privacy are particularly relevant to enquiries about individuals in hospitals or similar institutions.

Journalists themselves are no less strict. The National Union of Journalists' code of professional conduct says a journalist 'shall obtain information, photographs and illustrations only by straightforward means. The use of other means can be justified only by overriding considerations of the public interest'. It adds that, subject to that justification, 'a journalist shall do nothing which entails intrusion into private grief and distress'.

One thing to beware, though: a hospital manager will not get away with using patient confidentiality as a catch-all phrase to prevent journalists from making enquiries about patients, any more than the phrase *sub judice* can be used as a device to conceal information about the subject of quasi-legal inquiries and internal investigations.

COMPLAINTS AND INVESTIGATIONS ABOUT TREATMENT

In the case of complaints about a patient's treatment – usually made after the event, when either the patient is home again or something has gone seriously wrong – the same rules for patient confidentiality apply. The media should not be given any information about the patient which is not in the public domain.

If, however, the patient, or a relative or friend, is making inaccurate statements about treatment – for example, about the length of time the patient was kept waiting in the accident and emergency department – managers have the right to safeguard the interests of the hospital in responding, robustly if necessary. By going public, the patient has removed his or her right to protection over those aspects of care and treatment that have been put on record.

In many cases an official internal inquiry will already be underway. No statement should be made that anticipates the results of the inquiry. In circumstances where staff feel aggrieved at being publicly, and wrongly, criticized, it is legitimate to speak on their behalf to correct wrong facts, provided they are not crucial to the inquiry team's investigation.

Again, however, it must never be forgotten that the most important people in any investigation are the patient, family or friends. They have a right to be interviewed by journalists if they wish, to make their statements and to see the eventual inquiry report (possibly with some excisions if any passages relate to disciplinary aspects: staff have as much right to confidentiality as patients).

INFECTIOUS DISEASE OUTBREAK

The question sometimes arises: When is an infectious disease outbreak an outbreak? Doctors are scientifically trained, resistant to turning a handful of cases into a full-scale epidemic. But parents and other people think differently if a disease has, for example, killed a schoolchild and more than one case has occurred at the same school. It is better to put the cases into the public arena and into the right context than to wait for more to happen – or for a concerned parent to accuse the health authority or the education authority of a cover-up.

When an infectious disease breaks out, different organizations are involved: the district health authority, local authority and hospital all, at one stage or another, become the focus of media attention.

From the start, the health service person dealing with the media must define who he or she is working for and then make contact with counterparts in the other organizations, partly to maintain a common 'line' but also to ensure liaison.

A story about an outbreak of Legionnaire's disease, for example, will have the following aspects:

- the location of the outbreak (factory, office, hotel)

- the affected patients (at hospital or home)
- the disease control mechanism (consultant in communicable disease control, district health authority, laboratories)
- environmental health interest (local authority)
- safety at work (Health and Safety Executive).

Fast, accurate responses should be given on the health of affected patients and on the perceived danger to other residents or passersby. The aim should be to give the public generally, through the media, reliable, scientifically-based information about the disease, and to assist the media in following the detective work carried out by the public health team.

Equally complex arrangements apply in the case, for example, of a meningitis outbreak, where the concern of local parents adds a further dimension of anxiety to strengthen the media's stories. It is essential to try to get local newspapers and radio in particular to carry features and reports which explain the danger signals families should look out for, but also to make the point that scattered cases of meningitis do occur frequently, without being of epidemic proportions.

'Killer bug' stories are popular with national and local newspapers, and early information needs to be supplied to the media if the story is not to be exaggerated.

Deadlines – your opportunity

Newspapers will always be published on time and television and radio programmes broadcast on the dot. If their deadlines are seen by managers and public health doctors as an opportunity and not a threat, it is more likely that crucial messages will be communicated – particularly messages about preventive measures.

It may be difficult to persuade local radio stations to broadcast an item on meningitis in normal times, but when an outbreak has occurred they will beat a path to the health organization's door. A public health doctor who can talk well – and preferably one who has had media skills training – should be offered for interview on radio as soon as possible. The doctor can explain the symptoms, allay concerns and advise parents to see their GP with their children if they are worried. Such doctors, with all the authority that their job gives them in the minds of the public, can repeat the key messages on local television, with the communicable disease team working away in the community.

Radio and television are also, of course, extremely valuable if the experts are contact-tracing and need to find people who have been in a particular place at a particular time.

4

Codes of practice

The dividing lines between communicating too much and communicating too little are often blurred and uncertain. At the worst extremes, health service organizations may treat public information as if it were private, and journalists may treat private information as though it were public. For their part, doctors have to beware of overstepping ethical boundaries when they publicize their services.

Formal guidelines and codes of conduct exist to try to remove doubt and ambiguity. This chapter summarizes:

- a draft code of practice on openness for NHS trusts, district health authorities, family health services authorities, medical and dental practitioners and pharmacists

- guidance to doctors on advertising and publicizing their services

- codes of practice for journalists and broadcasters.

The NHS Executive's draft code of practice on openness (*see also* Chapter 1), issued for consultation in September 1994, largely reflected existing requirements and good practice. It said trusts and health authorities should make available:

- the details about important decisions on health policies, including the reasons for the decisions

- information to help people understand how the NHS deals with the public

- the reasons for decisions which may change the way services are delivered

- information about how health services are supplied, who is in charge and how people can complain, including how to contact the community health council and the Health Service Commissioner

- information about what services are supplied, the targets and standards that have been set, and the results achieved

- information about how people can get copies of their own health records.

INFORMATION WHICH MUST BE MADE PUBLIC BY NHS TRUSTS AND HEALTH AUTHORITIES

NHS trusts

These are statutorily required to publish by given dates each year:

- an annual report, describing the trust's performance over the previous financial year and including details of board members' remuneration

- a summary of the trust's business plan, describing its planned activity for the coming year

- a summary strategic direction document, setting out the trust's longer term plans for the delivery of health care services over a five-year period

- audited accounts.

There is no requirement to publish any of the above in draft or incomplete form or, in the case of the accounts, before they have been audited.

Trusts must make available, on request, the register of board members' private interests required under the Code of Accountability for NHS boards, and any information required under the *Patient's Charter*.

They are required to hold at least one public meeting a year.

District health authorities and family health services authorities

These organizations are required to prepare and make publicly available by given dates each year:

- an annual report, describing the performance over the previous financial year (with prescribed core content) and including details of board members' remuneration

- a report by the director of public health

- an annual report on performance against *Patient's Charter* rights and standards

- a full list of general medical practitioners, general dental practitioners, pharmacists and optometrists in their locality

- papers, agendas and minutes of board meetings held in public

- audited accounts.

Like trusts, they do not have to publish them in draft or incomplete form or, in the case of the accounts, before they have been audited.

They must produce, and make publicly available, a strategy document, setting out their plans over a five-year period. They should consult with the public before and after developing the strategy.

District health authorities and family health services authorities are required under the Public Bodies (Admission to Meetings) Act 1960 to hold all their board meetings in public. The agenda for these meetings must always be provided, on request, to the press.

District health authorities must consult with the community health council and other interested parties on any proposals which would result in a substantial change in the services which they provide to their residents.

OTHER TRUST AND HEALTH AUTHORITY INFORMATION WHICH SHOULD BE MADE AVAILABLE

NHS trusts

The draft code of practice recommended that NHS trusts should publish:

* quarterly board reports (financial, activity, quality and contract information)
* *Patient's Charter* performance against national targets and local performance against local targets
* information on service changes
* agenda, papers and minutes relating to the annual general meeting and any other meetings held in public.

Examples of information which should be made available by trusts to the public on request include:

* patient information leaflets
* description of facilities (numbers of beds, operating theatres, etc.)
* performance against *Patient's Charter* national and local standards and targets
* waiting times by specialty
* detailed information on activity
* broad conclusions of clinical audit

- number and percentage of operations cancelled, by specialty

- price lists for extra-contractual referrals

- information about clinicians (including qualifications, areas of special interest and waiting times for appointments)

- areas which have been, or are planned to be, market tested, with details of decisions reached and tenders received by value (not by the name of the tenderer)

- information on manpower and staffing levels, and staff salaries by broad bandings

- policies for trust staff (equal opportunities, standards of conduct, etc)

- environmental items (for example, fuel usage)

- tenders received by value

- volume and categories of complaints and letters of appreciation (without identifying individuals) and performance in handling complaints

- results of user surveys

- standing orders and waivers of standing orders

- standing financial instructions

- external audit management letter, and the trust's response, at the time when the response is made

- funds held on trust, such as bequests and donations.

Health authorities

Health authorities must make available on request:

- purchasing plans

- contracts with providers

- the register of the board members' private interests, required under the Code of Accountability for NHS boards

- such information as is required by the *Patient's Charter*.

Examples of information which should be considered for publication:

- leaflets (if available) describing services purchased by the authority

- information about consultation exercises undertaken, and outcomes

- outcomes of any user or attitude surveys

- total available financial resources

- district health authority allocation, adjusted to take account of such factors as age and general health of the local population (weighted capitation)

- proposed and actual expenditure on services, analysed by: providers, contracts (including by specialty, if available), and treatments purchased separately from contracts (extra-contractual referrals)

- analysis of changes in providers and contracts from previous years

- performance against quality standards in contracts

- clinical performance, by specialty, of contracted providers

- performance against national and local targets for in-patient and day case waiting times

- numbers of complaints dealt with, and response times

- names and contact (office) telephone numbers of board members and senior officers

- salaries of authority staff, by bandings, and in anonymized form.

Further examples of items of information that should be available to the public on request:

- future year resource plans

- any available information about expenditure on different types of health care, such as primary, secondary or community care

- price comparisons of all providers used by the purchaser

- total expenditure per head of population

- costs of authority administration

- standing orders and waivers of standing orders

- standing financial instructions

- external audit management letter and response, at the time when the response is made.

The draft code of practice gave additional guidance on examples of information that should be available from family health services authorities on request:

- expenditure on general medical services and prescribing

- average list size of general medical practices

- numbers of district nurses, health visitors and midwives attached to practices and number of practice nurses

- numbers of fundholding practices

- levels of immunization

- levels of screening for cervical cytology

- percentage of practices achieving top targets for smears and vaccinations

- achievement of health promotion targets

- information about types of premises (for example, health centres and branch surgeries)

- percentage of practices with GP practice charters

- initiatives to promote the work of primary care teams

- involvement of GPs in fundholding or in locality purchasing

- numbers and location of NHS dentists, including details of late opening and specialist services offered

- numbers and locations of pharmacists, and those offering:

    - late opening

    - oxygen supplies

    - supplies to residential homes

    - health promotion information

    - out-of-hours services for urgent prescriptions

    - needle exchange facilities

- numbers and locations of optometrists, and those offering late opening and domiciliary visits to carry out sight tests.

PRACTICE LEAFLETS

The draft code of practice set out the information which must be given in the practice leaflets of general medical and dental practitioners and pharmacists.

General medical practitioners (see also page 75)

Information must include:

- name, sex, medical qualifications, and date and first place of registration of the GP
- details of availability (including arrangements for when the GP is not available), the appointments system and how to obtain an urgent appointment or home visit
- arrangements for obtaining repeat prescriptions and dispensing arrangements
- frequency, duration and purpose of clinics
- numbers and roles of other staff employed by the practice, and information about whether the GP works alone, part-time or in partnership
- details of services available (child health surveillance, contraception, maternity medical, minor surgery, etc)
- details of arrangements for receiving patients' comments
- geographical boundary of the practice area
- details of access for people with disabilities.

Practice leaflets may also contain information about *Patient's Charter* standards.

General dental practitioners

Information must include:

- name, sex and date of registration as a dental practitioner

- address, opening hours and details of partners/associates

- whether a dental hygienist is employed

- details of access to the premises

- whether only orthodontic treatment is available

- with consent, whether the dentist speaks any languages in addition to English.

General dental practitioners are also required to display a notice of the scale of NHS charges.

Pharmacist

Pharmacists dispensing more than 1500 prescriptions a month normally produce practice leaflets detailing the range of service available to the public. These leaflets must contain:

- a list of services provided by the pharmacist

- name, address and telephone number of the pharmacy

- normal opening hours and arrangements for out-of-hours services and emergencies

- procedures for receiving comments on services provided.

Doctors

General practitioners are not only allowed to advertise their services but, as the previous section showed, have to provide practice leaflets giving information about their services.

The General Medical Council (GMC), in an official pamphlet, *Professional Conduct and Discipline: Fitness to Practise*, says:

> 'Good communication between doctors and patients, and between one doctor and another, is fundamental to the provision of good patient care, and those who need information about the services of doctors should have ready access to it. Patients need such information in order to make an informed choice of general practitioner and to make the best use of the services the general practitioner offers. Doctors, for their part, need information about the services of their professional colleagues.'

It adds, however, that patients are entitled to protection from misleading advertisements:

> 'The promotion of doctors' medical services as if the provision of medical care were no more than a commercial activity is likely both to undermine public trust in the medical profession and, over time, to diminish the standards of medical care which patients have a right to expect.'

Doctors who wish to offer medical services, such as medico-legal or occupational health services, or medical examinations, to a company or firm, a school or club, or a professional practitioner or association may send factual information about their qualifications and services to a suitable person, and may place a factual advertisement in a relevant trade journal.

The GMC says information about GPs should be made widely available to the public in areas where they practise. Specialists, however, may provide information to professional colleagues only and not to the public. The only exception is when a member of the public, seeking medical advice or treatment, approaches an association of doctors for a list of its members.

The main ways in which GPs can publicize their services are:

- through their own practice leaflets
- through the local media.

The British Medical Association (BMA), in *Medical Ethics Today: Its Practice and Philosophy*, has advised on both methods.

PRACTICE LEAFLETS

The BMA reminds GPs in the NHS that they are obliged, under their terms of service, to provide the public with information about their services in the form of a practice leaflet (see page 72). There is no such obligation on private practitioners.

The leaflet can be of any size or format. Doctors can feature a note about the partners' particular interests, such as child health, or their additional expertise, such as acupuncture or hypnotherapy. Photographs can be included.

Leaflets should not only be freely available in NHS surgeries, but can also be placed in libraries and advisory centres where prospective patients might look for health information.

Practice leaflets may be distributed in the area served by the practice to people who are, or who are not, patients of that practice, but advertising by means of unsolicited visits and/or telephone calls with the aim of recruiting patients is forbidden.

The BMA, though not the GMC, offers advice about commercial advertising in practice leaflets. It suggests that advertisements for local businesses should occupy no more than one third of the leaflet, which should clearly state that the practice is not endorsing the services advertised. The BMA advises against the inclusion of advertisements that might imply endorsement or recommendation – for example, advertisements for:

- products which clearly affect health adversely, such as tobacco products
- health-related services, such as pharmacies, nursing homes and private clinics.

But it sees no problems in doctors listing, for information, local pharmacies or health facilities.

MEDIA PUBLICITY

Factual information about GP services may be placed in the media, says the BMA. This may take the form of an advertisement, but the BMA has no objection to the information being given in the form of a brief article, as long as it conforms to the general advice on advertising and does not imply a superior service to that provided by other doctors. The type of information should reflect that required in practice leaflets and may include mention of health promotion clinics.

The BMA urges caution on newspaper features full of praise for a new surgery. These may be a form of secondary advertising for local businesses offering encouragement to the practice based there. Doctors must retain editorial control over any material advertising or alluding to their services, as they may be held responsible for the content.

Articles, books and broadcasting by doctors

The GMC gives the following advice:

'Books or articles written by doctors may include their names, qualifications, appointments and details of other publications. Similar information may be given where doctors participate in the broadcast presentation and discussion of medical and related topics. Difficulties in this area arise chiefly when material included in articles, books or broadcasts by doctors, or the manner in which it is referred to, is likely to imply that the doctor is especially recommended for patients to consult. Doctors should see to it that no such implication is given.

'Where a doctor in clinical practice writes articles or columns which offer advice to the public on medical conditions or problems, or offers telephone or other recorded advice on such subjects, or broadcasts about them, it should be explicitly stated that the doctor cannot offer individual advice or see individual patients as a result.'

ADVERTISING BY SPECIALISTS

A specialist's name, qualifications, address and telephone number can be included in local and national directories, but may not be distributed, unsolicited, to the public. Specialists are encouraged by the GMC to provide information to GPs and managerial colleagues, provided the information does not claim superiority for their personal qualities, qualifications, experience or skill.

The BMA has drawn attention to a dilemma for hospital specialists employed by NHS trusts. It points out that the financial prosperity of the trust is likely to depend increasingly on the quality of its staff, particularly the medical staff, and warns:

'The trust will therefore wish to advertise to its purchasers the particular merits of the specialists it employs... The opportunity for unethical behaviours is a very real one. Doctors should be vigilant in ensuring that any advertising material circulated by health service trusts conforms explicitly and implicitly with the GMC guidelines.'

Journalists and broadcasters

Journalists in newspapers, magazines, radio and television work under strict, largely self-imposed, codes of practice. The National Union of Journalists (NUJ) has its own code of professional conduct in which it states that journalists will at all times defend the principle of the freedom of the press and other media in relation to the collection of information and the expression of comment and criticism. It adds, among other principles, that journalists 'shall obtain information, photographs and illustrations only by straightforward means' unless justified by overriding consideration of public interest (see footnote on page 79).

Codes of practice exist for the newspaper and magazine industry and for broadcasting companies. The main ones are those issued by the Press Complaints Commission and the Independent Television Commission. The BBC has strict internal guidelines for journalists and producers of factual programmes.

THE PRESS COMPLAINTS COMMISSION

The newspaper and magazine industry drew up a code of practice in 1991, parts of which are particularly relevant to health services and patients. The code, ratified by the Press Complaints Commission, says that all members of the press have a duty:

* to maintain the highest professional and ethical standards
* to safeguard the public's right to know.

The Commission, whose members are drawn from the public and the press, is an independent organization that ensures British newspapers and magazines follow the letter and spirit of the code. It receives, and adjudicates on, complaints about possible breaches of the code and gives general advice to editors on ethical issues. The code does not apply to advertisements, broadcast material, or the contents of books, leaflets or pamphlets.

The code of practice includes the following clauses.

Accuracy

— Newspapers and magazines should take care not to publish inaccurate, misleading or distorted material.

— Whenever it is recognized that a significant inaccuracy, misleading statement or distorted report has been published, it should be corrected promptly and with due prominence.

— An apology should be published whenever appropriate.

— A newspaper or periodical should always report fairly and accurately the outcome of an action for defamation to which it has been a party.

Opportunity to reply

— A fair opportunity for reply to inaccuracies should be given to individuals or organizations when reasonably called for.

Comment, conjecture and fact

— Newspapers, while free to be partisan, should distinguish clearly between comment, conjecture and fact.

Privacy

— Intrusions and enquiries into an individual's private life without his or her consent, including the use of long-lens photography to take pictures of people on private property[1] without their consent, are not generally acceptable, and publication can only be justified when in the public interest[2].

---

[1] The Commission defines 'private property' as including those parts of a hospital or nursing home where patients are treated or accommodated.

[2] In the Commission's definition of 'public interest', newspapers and magazines are serving the public interest when: detecting or exposing crime or a serious misdemeanour; protecting public health and safety; or preventing the public from being misled by a statement or action of an individual or organization.

Listening devices

— Unless justified by public interest, journalists should not obtain or publish material obtained by using clandestine listening devices or by intercepting private telephone conversations.

Hospitals

— Journalists or photographers making enquiries at hospitals or similar institutions should identify themselves to a responsible executive and obtain permission before entering non-public areas.

— The restrictions on intruding into privacy are particularly relevant to enquiries about individuals in hospitals or similar institutions.

Misrepresentation

— Journalists should not generally obtain or seek to obtain information or pictures through misrepresentation or subterfuge.

— Unless in the public interest, documents or photographs should be removed only with the express consent of the owner.

— Subterfuge can be justified only in the public interest and only when material cannot be obtained by any other means.

Harassment

— Journalists should neither obtain nor seek to obtain information or pictures through intimidation or harassment.

— Unless their enquiries are in the public interest, journalists should not photograph individuals on private property (including that defined above, under 'Privacy') without their consent; should not persist in telephoning or questioning individuals after having been asked to desist; should not remain on their property after having been asked to leave, and should not follow them.

Intrusion into grief or shock

— In cases involving personal grief or shock, enquiries should be carried out and approaches made with sympathy and discretion.

Interviewing or photographing children

— Journalists should not normally interview or photograph children under the age of 16 on subjects involving the personal welfare of the child, in the absence of, or without the consent of, a parent or other adult who is responsible for the children.

Confidential sources

— Journalists have a moral obligation to protect confidential sources of information.

THE INDEPENDENT TELEVISION COMMISSION

The Commission's programme code gives guidance to independent television companies on a wide range of matters relating to conduct and standards. Among them are the following:

Filming and recording in institutions

— When permission is received to film or record material in an institution, such as a hospital...which has regular dealings with the public, but which would not normally be accessible to cameras without such permission, it is very likely that the material will include shots of individuals who are themselves incidental, not central, figures in the programme.... As a general rule, no obligation to seek agreement arises when the appearance of the persons shown is incidental and they are clearly random and anonymous members of the general public.

— On the other hand, when their appearance is not incidental, and they are not random and anonymous members of the public, a producer should seek specific consent. Any exceptions should be justifiable in the public interest.

— When by reason of disability or infirmity a person is not in a position either to give or to withhold agreement, permission to use the material should be sought from the next-of-kin or from the person responsible for their care.

Recorded telephone interviews

— Interviews or conversations conducted by telephone should not normally be recorded for inclusion in a programme or in the course of preparation for a programme unless the interviewer has identified himself or herself...and described the general purpose of the programme and the interviewee has given consent to the use of the conversation in the programme.

Scenes of extreme suffering and distress

— Scenes of human suffering and distress are often an integral part of any report of the effects of natural disaster, accident or human violence, and may be a proper subject for direct portrayal rather than indirect reporting. But before presenting such scenes a producer needs to balance the wish to serve the needs of truth and the desire for compassion against the risk of sensationalism and the possibility of an unwarranted invasion or privacy.

— The individual's right to privacy at times of bereavement or extreme distress must in particular be respected.

— Insensitive questioning not only risks inflicting additional distress on the interviewee, but also offends many viewers.

Factual programmes – news

— Any news, given in whatever form, must be presented with due accuracy and impartiality. Reporting should be dispassionate and news judgements based on the need to give viewers an even-handed account of events.

Conduct of interviews

— Interviewees should be made adequately aware of the format, subject matter and purpose of the programme to which they have been invited to contribute and the way in which their contribution is likely to be used. Written confirmation should be provided if requested.

— For programmes dealing with political or industrial controversy or current public policy, interviewees should also be told the identity and intended role of other proposed participants in the programme, where this is known.

— On occasion, proposed interviewees will be unable or unwilling to accept an invitation to participate in a programme. This need not prevent the programme going out...but care must be taken to given an impartial account of the subject under discussion.... Reference to the absence of such a spokesman should be made in as detached and factual manner as possible.

Editing of interviews

— Impartiality applies equally to the editing of interviews. Editing to shorten recorded interviews must not distort or misrepresent the known views of the interviewee.

Complaints from viewers

— Where it feels a complaint is justified, the Commission will take action with the television company concerned.

For information

More information can be obtained from:

The Independent Television Commission
70 Brompton Road
London SW3 1EY
Telephone: 0171 584 7011

HOW TO COMPLAIN TO THE PRESS COMPLAINTS COMMISSION AND THE BROAD-CASTING COMPLAINTS COMMISSION

1 The Press Complaints Commission

The Press Complaints Commission usually deals only with complaints from people and organizations directly affected by the matters about which they complain. It will consider complaints from people not directly affected by the material published when there is a breach of the code which significantly affects the public interest and has not been resolved previously.

The Commission is best able to deal with complaints while the circumstances are fresh in everyone's mind, and will usually accept only complaints made within one month of either the publication date or the editor's reply to a complaint.

People are advised to write first to the editor and give the newspaper or magazine at least seven days to reply. If the matter is not settled in this way, or the person complaining is dissatisfied with the response, a letter should be sent to the Commission, with a dated copy of the item being complained about and copies of any relevant correspondence.

Nearly all complaints and adjudications are dealt with on paper. The Commission accepts only those complaints which can be resolved under the code of practice.

It sends every letter which raises a *prima facie* breach of the code to the editor with a request to attempt a swift resolution of the difficulty. If the complaint cannot be resolved directly in this way, a report will be considered at a monthly meeting of the Commission. All the relevant documents are collated with a draft adjudication which the Commission will discuss and accept or amend. Neither complainants nor representatives of publications will be asked to attend.

When the Commission has adjudicated, it will send a copy of its adjudication to all parties before it is published in the Commission's monthly report. It will require the newspaper or magazine to publish its adjudication when a complaint has been upheld.

Full information about the code of practice (summarized on pages 78/81) and how to complain can be obtained from:

The Press Complaints Commission
1 Salisbury Square
London EC4Y 3AE
Telephone: 0171 353 1248
Fax: 0171 353 8355

Press Complaints Commission Helpline

The Press Complaints Commission has a special Helpline (0171 353 3732) to advise people who believe the code of practice is likely to be breached in respect of their own affairs. The Helpline will give basic information about the publication or news agency involved and the name, address, telephone and fax numbers of the relevant editor so that complainants may get speedily in touch.

2 The Broadcasting Complaints Commission

The Broadcasting Complaints Commission is an independent statutory body set up by the Home Secretary in 1981 to consider and adjudicate on certain types of complaint about radio and television programmes. It will consider complaints of:

- unjust or unfair treatment in radio or television programmes actually broadcast or included in a licensed cable or satellite programme service

- unwarranted infringement of privacy in, or in connection with the obtaining of material included in, such programmes.

Who can complain?

Complaints may be made by individuals or organizations.

Complaints of unjust or unfair treatment must be made by someone who was a participant in the programme, or has a direct interest in the treatment of which they complain (or by someone authorized to complain on their behalf). It is not enough that an individual should simply feel that a subject was not fairly treated or that a programme was unbalanced or misleading. There must be some direct personal interest.

Complaints of unwarranted infringement of privacy must be made by the person whose privacy was infringed (or by someone authorized to complain on their behalf).

The Commission may consider a complaint made on behalf of someone who has died, provided the programme in question was broadcast within five years of the death.

How to complain

Complaints must be made in writing. They may be made direct to the Commission or after a complainant has complained to the broadcasters and is not satisfied with the response.

Complainants should write to the Secretary of the Commission, giving the title of the programme and the date and channel on which it was broadcast. They should explain in what way they consider the programme was unjust or unfair, or in what way they consider their privacy was unwarrantedly infringed.

What happens when a complaint is received

The Commission decides whether the complaint is within its jurisdiction. It will not entertain, or proceed with, a complaint if it appears that:

- the unjust or unfair treatment or the unwarranted infringement of privacy complained of is the subject of legal proceedings

- the complainant has a remedy by way of legal proceedings and, in the particular circumstances, it is inappropriate for the Commission to entertain the complaint

- the complaint is frivolous or, for any other reason, it is inappropriate for the Commission to deal with it.

What happens when a complaint is to be considered further

If the Commission decides to entertain a complaint, it sends a copy to the broadcasters and requires them to provide a transcript of the programme and a written statement in answer to the complaint.

The Commission may give the complainant the opportunity to respond in writing to this statement. The response is sent to the broadcasters, who may be invited to make a further written statement. The Commission may also invite the complainant and representatives of the broadcasters, together or separately, to appear before the Commission members to answer questions.

The Commission sets out its findings in a written adjudication.

What happens after the Commission has adjudicated

Copies of the adjudication and a summary are sent to the complainant and the broadcasters. Whether or not the complaint has been upheld, the Commission normally directs the broadcasters to broadcast the summary, and publish it in the *Radio Times* or *TV Times* as appropriate. The Commission cannot require the broadcasters to apologize to the complainant, broadcast a correction or provide a financial remedy.

Further information about the Commission can be obtained from:

The Secretary,
The Broadcasting Complaints Commission
Grosvenor Gardens House
35/37 Grosvenor Gardens
London SW1W 0BS
Telephone: 0171 630 1966

5

Writing to be read

Probably the most time-consuming activity in the health service is putting words on paper. A far less common activity is reading the words that others have written. The difference between the two poses an obvious question: Why is so much time and effort being wasted on sending out messages that do not get through?

Take, for instance, leaflets by GPs for their patients. In 1992, Tim Albert and Stephanie Chadwick subjected 79 practice leaflets to a readability test. They reported in the *British Medical Journal* that 13% of the leaflets had readability scores comparable to those of a medical journal rather than those of a daily newspaper. How likely are the leaflets to be widely read?

Then there are medical journals themselves. How many doctors read them and change their professional decisions accordingly? Researchers are now examining this subject, but commercial surveys have shown for some time that GPs, for example, are far more likely to get their information from other sources.

As for managers, what does this sentence mean: 'Plans for service development must be client-focused with a clear goal of providing integrated and seamless care for all those who use our services...'? Delegates at a conference intended to sell the idea of marketing to sceptical doctors were bombarded with phrases like 'quasi-customer marketing interface' and 'the provider agenda is essentially quality-driven'. A Government press release on the *Patient's Charter* was harder to read than the charter it was describing. Both, however, were on the same level as a heavy editorial in a broadsheet newspaper.

Some organizations use writing to convey undiluted success and self-satisfaction instead of simple messages of fact and opinion. They produce documents that are designed to be touched and admired, but not to be read. Glossy brochures, printed on several different types of expensive paper, have strings of long words beautifully arranged in trendy, tiny typefaces around artful photographs taken with a fish-eye lens.

There is another trend: the pompous initial capital letter. The College of Hypochondriacs would be a proper noun and rightly deserve a capital. Thereafter, however, 'the college' should take its place with other common nouns and a lower case 'c'. In practice, its governing body would probably insist on being 'the College' with a capital 'C'. Yet capital letters are notoriously hard to read. They also send out a message that this word (or person or organization) is important. The survey of practice leaflets, mentioned above, exposed many cases of 'Doctors', 'Nurses' and 'Practice Managers'. With one exception, 'patients' had a small 'p'.

Capital letters may inflate Important People and small letters (however accidentally) may appear to demote relatively unimportant people. But language can exclude people so that only members of the same 'club' can understand what is going on. The newer the profession, the greater the need for such vocabulary. Not so long ago, hospital administrators would regularly lampoon doctors for their jargon. Now doctors regularly lampoon the administrators – or, rather, the managers – because their documents teem with words like 'seamless care' and 'empowerment'. However, this fight detracts from the real battle, which is to remind all groups of the true purpose of this kind of writing.

Five principles contain the most important lessons that can point the way to clarity in written communication:

- Know what you are saying, to whom you are saying it, and why you are saying it.
- Start with the most important part of the message.
- Make the subject of the action the subject of the sentence.
- Write in language your audience will understand.
- Watch out for the basics.

KNOW WHAT YOU ARE SAYING, TO WHOM YOU ARE SAYING IT, AND WHY YOU ARE SAYING IT

Writers often fail to communicate because they have failed to make their purpose clear. No single message comes across. Writers can put across a clear message only if they bother to work out the message in the first place.

Too often, we go straight to the word processor. We write. We then move blocks of text around to impose some kind of order. When we have finished, a clear message may, or may not, have emerged.

Even if we do try to work out our message in advance, we often think only of the subjects (ie the nouns) and not what happened to them (as expressed in a verb). 'St Anne's Hospital and long waiting lists', for instance, fails to state whether St Anne's 'has', 'has not', 'should have' or 'hasn't a chance of reducing' waiting lists. Each change will take the writing in a different direction and deciding this route in advance will give the writer a reasonable chance of arriving at the most suitable destination.

The second part of the principle is 'Know for whom you are writing'. This is vital, but often overlooked, or fudged, with disastrous results. All readers share some common characteristics: they are busy; they are anxious for an excuse to stop reading; they have far too much to read; and they are selfish. But otherwise they have enormous differences in vocabulary, background knowledge, motivation, time, ability and concentration. Thus the more specifically you can define your audience, the greater the chance of getting your message across.

This is where problems start to appear. Is the press release on a £1 million research grant being written for the reporter on the local newspaper or is it to impress the academics who will be doing the work? Is the internal report being written for the head of department who will approve it, or the members of the board who have to make a decision? Who is the target reader for the annual report of the director of public health? Being clear on this – and resisting the temptation to write for more than one group – will again reduce the chances of failure.

There is a dangerous distraction. When we write, we usually receive our feedback from the wrong people. GPs writing a leaflet for patients will pass the draft to their partners. As the partners read it, they will make changes according to their own personal agendas, knowledge and styles. Each time, the document will become less intelligible to those for whom it was originally intended.

The third part of the principle is that writers must be clear, before they start writing, not only about *what* and *to whom*, but also *why*. This introduces the concept of political writing, which is when the writer, quite legitimately, wants to make his or her writing unclear. It is acceptable to write a document entirely in management rococo, redolent with the latest technical vocabulary, if the intention is to show that you have been to all the right seminars. Similarly, it is acceptable to break some of the guidelines under the following principles in this section, if you wish to distance yourself from the action, as in: 'The job has been terminated' ('You're fired') or 'This is not a success' ('You're a failure').

Do not automatically spray thickets of dense prose with Plain English weed-killer. But do not fail to communicate by default.

START WITH THE MOST IMPORTANT PART OF THE MESSAGE

Health care professionals often complain that their writing is boring, and they ask for ways of 'livening it up'. The solution rests as much on structures as on style. We may criticize the tabloid press for many of the types of stories they use. However, we should not criticize them for the way these stories are presented, because they make excellent models of effective communication.

One important technique is based on the journalist's recognition that the newspapers have to fight for their readers. They unashamedly use the first sentence as a hook on the grounds that if it fails to work, they will have failed. Scientific writers, on the other hand, reverse this process. This is because for several decades journals have favoured the IMRAD formula: Introduction (Why did we start?), Methods (What did we do?), Results (What did we find?) and Discussion (What does it mean?).

Authors of a scientific paper must honour this convention, but for all other types of writing they should make the most interesting part stand in its proper place – up front. A newsletter contained an article that started with the following paragraph:

'The Secretary of State, Virginia Bottomley, recently announced her intention to introduce as part of an extension of the Patient's Charter a new target, so that patients waiting for coronary artery bypass grafts are admitted within 12 months. It is understood that the policy will also include coronary angioplasty, although that was not said in the initial announcement. The Association has identified the need to cover other forms of heart disease, including paediatric cases, within an approach to treating heart disease and the Patient's Charter.'

A more reader-friendly alternative would have been:

'Coronary bypass grafts and coronary angioplasty are not the only procedures that should be included in the targets for the *Patient's Charter*,
according to the Association...'.

As shown above, scientifically trained writers extend the IMRAD
structure to paragraphs, so that they start by setting the scene and
tuck the main point away at the end. This runs counter to standard
advice, which puts a 'topic sentence' outlining the main point at the
start of each paragraph.

Even sentences start to follow this pattern. Take this passage:
'Following a review of information available from our statistical
returns, and a resolution of the last unit care meeting, I would ask you
to note that all home visits to customers of our service should be by
appointment only.'

It needs to be split into two sentences, and the second sentence
moved up to become the first: 'All home visits by staff of the unit will
be by appointment only. This follows a decision at a meeting...'.

MAKE THE SUBJECT OF THE ACTION THE SUBJECT OF THE SENTENCE

Another curious aspect of managerial and scientific writing is that it
often uses the passive voice. Thus 'surveys are administered' and 'closure of the hospital is agreed'. For political writing this may be useful,
but unfortunately its use has grown so that many people feel that a
sentence is badly constructed unless it is written in that way.

The reverse is true. The passive can cause sentences to go seriously awry, mainly by taking the subject out of its proper place and
hiding it away. Take this sentence: 'Although concern about the
impact of current housing and public health was shown by a substantial number of directors, the main activity was still allocation of
increasing housing need and homelessness.' What does it mean?
Finding the real subject of the sentence – and starting with it – does
at least allow for a good attempt: 'Housing need and homelessness are
increasing, even though many directors of public health are worried
about the effect of them on health.'

A related convention insists that writers should never use the first person. 'I' or 'we'. Again, there is no problem if there is a sound political reason for hiding the fact that you have done something. But usually this convention arises from false modesty and a lingering belief that it is 'good style'. It is not: there is, after all, a wealth of difference between 'it is believed' and 'I believe'.

WRITE IN LANGUAGE YOUR AUDIENCE WILL UNDERSTAND

One of the hardest tasks is trying to persuade people to use simple language. They still feel that when they sit at their word processor, or when they dictate their report or letter, they have to use different words and constructions from those they would normally use when talking to the same kind of people, at home or in the pub.

If we want to get a message across, then the highest virtue is simplicity.

First, do not use a long word if a short one will do. 'Start' and 'stop' will usually be more effective than 'commence' and 'terminate'. Readers are unlikely to condemn you as ill-read; they should be far too busy reading what you have written.

Second, do not use several words if one will do. 'Patients prefer the treatment, and it's cheaper' is more effective than 'It has been established that the curtailed treatment schedule may offer perceived social advantages for patients, with the additional benefit of it being more economical'. Being sparing with words also helps to avoid such embarrassments as 'two-way dialogue' or 'fully comprehensive'.

Third, do not hide the fact that you are writing about people. Let boys be 'boys' and not 'male paediatric patients'. Write 'more psychiatrists' rather than 'additional consultant medical staff within psychiatry'. Let people 'walk about' and not force them to be 'ambulatory out-patient cases'.

Finally, avoid what a famous editor, Harold Evans, called 'monologophobia'. This is the pathological fear of having the same word appear twice within two thousand words of itself. A report can be called a report throughout; to call it a 'report' in line one, a 'study' in line four, and an 'investigation' in line six is confusing.

WATCH OUT FOR THE BASICS

Some people use grammar as a stick to beat anyone else who dares to write words and sentences other people want to read. These critics will point out where you have split an infinitive, started a sentence with 'and' or 'but', or ended with a preposition. It is pointless to give them the references in modern books of usage that say that all three are now permitted. If you do, they will see it as yet another example of the decline of Western civilization.

The English language lives and develops. Even the words change. 'Partial' used to mean 'biased towards' or 'in favour of'. Now we happily talk about 'partially opened borders'. Strictly speaking, 'more than' should be used for numbers and 'over' for quantities, but, again, the distinction has disappeared. (It does, however, cause difficulties, as in the airline boast, 'We serve over 50 cities'.)

There are three areas in which writers still need to get the basics right.

The first is spelling. Dr Bernard Lamb, of Imperial College, London, discovered that his nursing students were confusing 'elevate' with 'alleviate' and 'proscribe' with 'prescribe'. Patients would be right to be alarmed!

The instruction on a packet of pills, 'Take two days running, then skip a day', is asking for trouble.

The second is punctuation, and particularly the use of the comma. A press release from a teaching hospital contained this sentence: 'Anyone who is concerned about the speech and language, or swallowing of a family member, or themselves, is welcome to attend one of the open days.'

The third area is the constant need to use commonsense. 'Centre around' is obviously illogical. 'Seamless care' which 'dovetails' is, as any carpenter will confirm, an impossibility. The instruction on a packet of pills, 'take two days running, then skip a day' is asking for trouble.

The best way of avoiding such errors is to test your writing on some of your intended readers. It may sometimes be humiliating, but your writing will be the better for it.

It will be a reminder that you are writing for the readers, not for yourself.

6

Products, events and programmes

Many of the techniques of public relations have been described as they relate to staff, opinion formers and the news media. These and more general communications need to be reinforced by products such as journals and exhibitions, programmes such as campaigns to win support for change, and events such as public meetings. Some events celebrate achievement and involve leading figures – members of the Royal Family or the Government, for example.

Whether they are major or modest, products, programmes and events all need to be planned and implemented carefully if they are to be successful, with nothing left to chance. This chapter goes through the nuts and bolts of the work involved in:

* journals

* exhibitions and audio-visual aids

* events and meetings

* Royal visits and other ceremonial occasions

* public relations campaigns

* health promotion programmes.

Throughout all of these, health service managers should take account of the needs of people with cultural differences or language difficulties. Will special attention need to be given to the wording and to possible translation? If some readers or audiences are visually impaired, will the use of helpers, sign language, Braille or audio-tape versions need to be considered?

Journals

A 'journal', whether in the form of a newsletter, newspaper, magazine or one-page bulletin, can communicate important information in an accessible, attractive and relevant way. It can:

- aid understanding and agreement by explaining and illustrating complicated policy issues

- reach large numbers of people for relatively little cost

- help build a sense of pride in an organization

- foster a common sense of identity among people working in different parts and at different levels of an organization

- inform, educate and entertain.

Thousands of journals – weekly photocopied bulletins, monthly two-colour newsletters, tabloid style newspapers and full-colour magazines – are produced every year by health service organizations. They may be produced for all the staff in the organization, for certain groups of staff, for GPs, for opinion formers, for carers, or for the public at large.

Some are successful long-running publications, eagerly awaited by their readers. Others are turgid vehicles of management-speak, lacking credibility. Some try to compensate for inadequate content by over-design – victims, possibly, of the enthusiastic but untrained operator of the office computer's new desktop publishing package. Many start with good intentions but fade away by Issue 3.

A journal has its limitations. The communications flow is mainly one-way, despite feedback mechanisms such as readership surveys and letters pages. And no matter how effective, a journal is only part of the organization's communications effort. It cannot resolve all the communications challenges an organization faces and does not absolve managers from the responsibility of talking and listening to their staff and other key audiences.

So what can be done to ensure the journal is an effective tool of communication? The first step is to define its:

- objectives
- target audience
- editorial policy.

OBJECTIVES

Clear objectives are essential. There is a world of difference between a journal that provides information only and one that is intended to provoke debate. The internal newsletter of an NHS trust might have as its objectives:

- to communicate with all staff about the trust's plans, policies and actions
- to foster a common sense of purpose throughout the trust
- to celebrate the achievements of the trust and its staff
- to provide a forum for discussion and debate about the policies of the trust.

TARGET READERSHIP

The target readership could be all staff or a group of staff, such as junior doctors. It could be a whole community, reached by door-to-door distribution, or a specific group in the community, such as informal carers. There may be secondary target audiences: a newsletter for staff can also be sent to local opinion formers or the local news media as a source of positive stories.

The editor needs to understand and take into account the target audience's perceptions and experiences. He or she does so through a combination of formal research (focus groups and surveys), informal contacts, and 'gut instinct'. It can help to build a picture of the typical reader: a senior physiotherapist, perhaps, or the vice-chairman of a community health council.

EDITORIAL POLICY

A journal must have an editor – a single editor who is responsible for pulling together the whole publication. Editing by committee does not work.

Lines of accountability must be clear. Does the editor have to show the final text to an 'editor-in-chief' (for example, the chief executive) before it goes to print, or is the editor's decision final?

Ideally, the editor should be given a free hand to produce a journal which, by presenting a balanced, accurate picture, has credibility with both the 'owners' (the health service organization) and the target readership. It may require courage to give an editor freedom to print stories which contain a third party's criticism of the organization or its policies, but the alternative is a management journal which lacks credibility and thus fails to convince.

Editorial freedom also brings responsibilities. The editor must ensure that the journal reflects the aims and direction of the organization, and that its editorial policy – on racist or sexist language, for example – is in line with the organization's own policies.

Once objectives, target audience and editorial policy are agreed, the editor needs to work through six practical questions:

- What resources are available?

- What will the journal contain and how will the contents be gathered?

- How often will it be published?

- What will it look like?

- How will it be produced?

- How will it reach the target audience?

Resources

As well as establishing a budget for production costs, the editor needs to assess the staff time and the skills that will be required.

Editorial time should not be underestimated. An editor who already has a full and demanding job cannot be expected to edit a journal during the lunch-break or at the end of the day. Editors and contributors may need training to ensure they use the available time in the most effective ways.

An editor who already has a full and demanding job cannot be expected to edit a journal during the lunch break.

How much flexibility is there in the overall budget? It may be worth cutting print costs by reducing the number of pages or any colour used and using the money to buy in specialist help to make the journal readable.

One way of reducing the budgeted cost of the journal is to include paid-for advertisements. However, the editor must ensure that any extra income received is worth the effort expended. Looking for advertisers, writing advertising copy, checking design and layout, vetting the content, collecting fees and ensuring advertisers meet copy deadlines can be time-consuming and frustrating. Such tasks are often best left to the expertise of an advertising agency.

Content

Most journals will contain a mixture of news and feature items. The editor will draw on a number of sources including national stories about health issues, briefings with senior managers, policy documents, agendas and the grapevine. He or she needs a good sense of what makes news, and has to develop the news sense of the colleagues and other contacts who supply information. It may be worth identifying local 'reporters' in each area who have responsibility for spotting and supplying news.

In staff journals, regular items include diaries of forthcoming events, starters and leavers, health promotion news, letters from readers and competitions. Contributions from other members of staff should be welcomed, not least because they encourage a sense of ownership.

Journal contributors should be given guidelines on style and presentation of copy (typed and double-spaced is best) and should be rewarded with bylines (their name mentioned). But the editor should make it clear that he or she reserves the right to cut stories to fit or to make sense – and that the editor's decision is final.

The editor may also decide that a news or feature story would benefit from an independent perspective. A freelance reporter's fly-on-the-wall account of a day in the life of a health visitor, for example, will probably yield more insights than an account of the same day written after the event by the health visitor.

Editors and reporters should follow these simple rules of structure and style:

- Get the main point in the first paragraph.

- Get the facts right.

- Keep the language clear, unambiguous and readable.

- Distinguish between fact and comment.

- Follow a set house-style.

Get the main point in the first paragraph

Every story needs a news angle – a 'hook' (as described in Chapter 5) on which hangs the rest of the story. It needs to grab the attention of the reader. Bureaucrats are taught to structure reports with an introduction, case for, case against, and conclusion. News stories turn that order on the head and put the conclusion in the first paragraph.

Compare the following two story openings:

'A sub-group of the control of infection committee was set up in September 1993. Its terms of reference were to investigate the current use of sharps boxes on the wards, to identify any necessary improvements in procedures, and to make recommendations to that effect...'

'Staff are risking infection by not putting needles in the sharps boxes provided, an expert committee has found. The trust is to launch an intensive training programme to show staff how to dispose of needles safely...'

Every reporter is taught to answer in the opening sentences the questions: Who? What? Where? When? Why? How? Giving information in order of importance also allows a story to be cut from the bottom if it is too long for the space allocated.

Get the facts right

Accuracy is essential. That means getting not just half the story, but all the story, and getting the right names, titles, addresses, ages, dates and figures. It also means checking and double-checking.

Keep the language clear, unambiguous and readable

Avoid long words where shorter or simpler ones will do the same job. Do not assume that readers, even senior health service staff, know the meaning of all health service jargon. Keep sentences and paragraphs short and use the active form rather than the passive wherever possible.

Distinguish between fact and comment

Comment makes a story come to life, but it must be attributed. The new rapid diagnostic centre may well be an exciting and imaginative venture which will change the face of local health care, but that comment should be made within quotation marks by the chairman or chief executive and not by the journal itself.

Such words as 'radical' and 'innovative' in an opening paragraph or headline are acceptable, provided they are attributed early in the story. Only in an editorial column (in which the editor expresses a particular viewpoint) should the journal speak directly to its readers.

Follow a set house-style

An agreed house-style saves time spent editing and gives the publication a reassuringly consistent feel. It should cover common aspects such as the use of initial capitals (avoid where possible), where abbreviations are acceptable, which numbers are spelt out (ten but 11?), and whether first names are used.

Frequency

Frequency of publication depends on the nature of the journal and the resources available. A fast-news staff bulletin may need to be published once or twice a week. A magazine-style journal, perhaps aimed at a mainly external readership and with more features than news, may be published monthly, every two months or quarterly.

The frequency must be achievable within given resources. It is better to start with a quarterly journal which becomes monthly when resources allow than to launch a monthly journal which fails to appear on time.

Whatever the chosen frequency, every journal needs a production schedule with deadlines for each stage of the process. A typical schedule for an eight-page journal, appearing every two months, would be as follows:

March 1995 edition

13 January	Initial list of items drawn up; articles and photographs commissioned.
6 February	Deadline for all submitted copy (ie the text from contributors).
13 February	Start page layout of edited copy.
22 February	Final copy to printers.
28 February	Delivery and distribution.

Design

Every journal uses design features, such as page layout and fonts (typefaces), to create its own visual identity. Its identity should be determined by its objectives: a fast-news bulletin will probably use simple page layouts and a basic font; an opinion formers' magazine may have a more complex page layout and a more adventurous font.

A graphic designer can be briefed to create the design for the publication. But if your budget is very tight, you can create your own. Either way, it should take into account the following factors:

Structure

Based on the contents that you have decided on, a master flat plan should be drawn up to show what each page will contain (see Figure 3).

Size of paper

Newsletters tend to be A4 size, or occasionally A3. Large-circulation journals in newspaper format are often printed on local newspaper presses and are usually tabloid size (the size of the *Daily Mail* or *Daily Mirror*).

Font

An easy-to-read font of a reasonable size should be used. It is best to use one font only for the main text and another one, usually in a larger size, for the headlines. Variety can be achieved in headlines with the use of capitals, upper and lower case, and italics, but the effect should be attractive and clear, not cluttered and 'busy'.

Masthead

This will include the organization's logo, the name of the publication, date and issue number, and a brief line to explain the journal's purpose.

Page layout

The basic building block for the layout is the number of columns per page. The more columns, the more complicated the layout. Most A4 newsletters use two or three columns; a tabloid-size newspaper may use five or six.

For variety, text and headlines can be set across two or three columns, and other devices such as tints, rules, boxes and pictures can be used.

Every page should have a focus. The reader's eye should be drawn to the main story, then to the next most important story and so on, across and down the page. Alternatively, the main focus may be a photograph.

The freedom of centre-page spreads can be used for features, with pictures and headlines across the two pages.

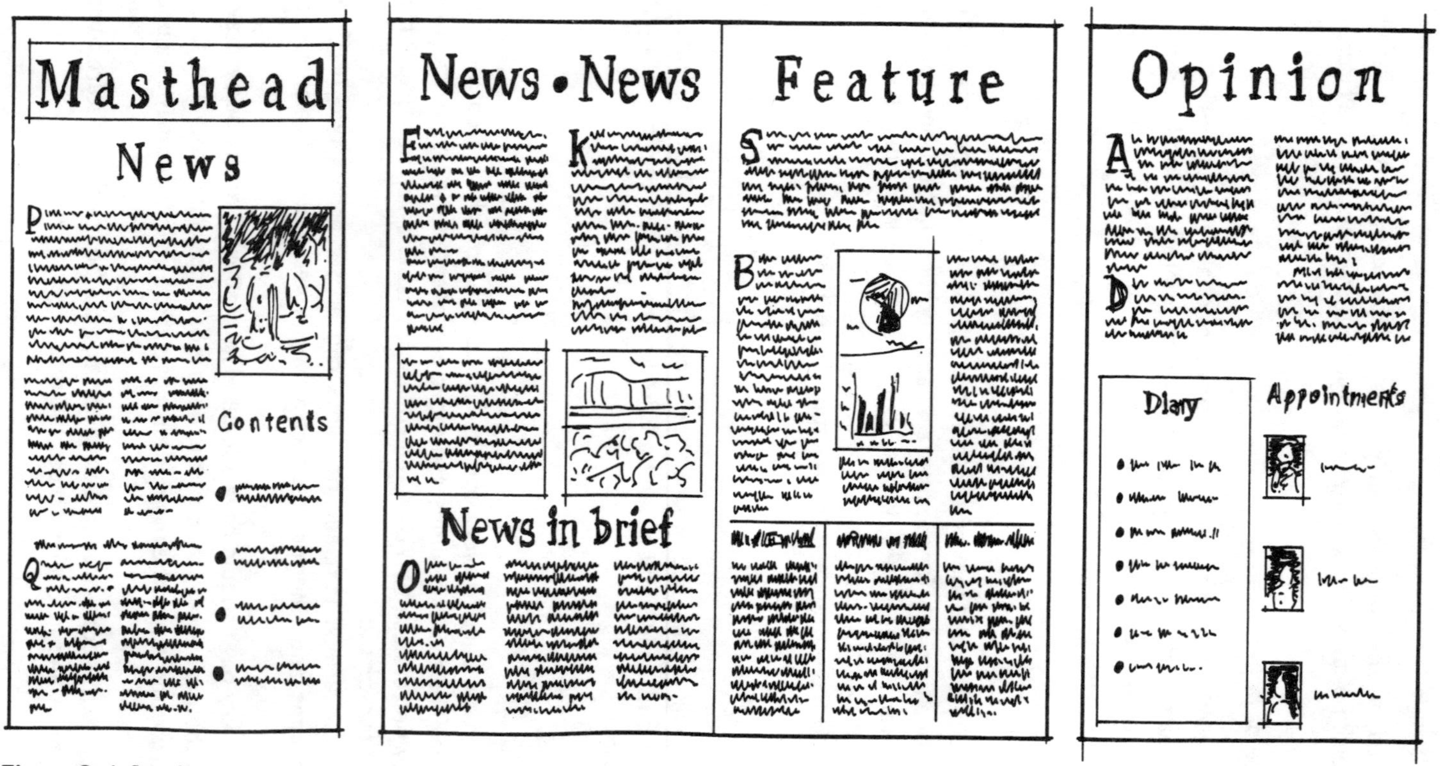

Figure 3: A flat plan

Photographs and illustrations

Photographs and illustrations help bring the page layouts to life.

Many news stories can be made more interesting with a photograph. Look for unusual or spectacular picture opportunities, such as the delivery by crane of the CT scanner to the X-ray department on the sixth floor. If the league of friends has paid for some life-saving equipment, show not only the cheque presentation but also the equipment in use.

Remember that, generally, buildings are boring and people are fascinating.

Photographs of individual people should usually be no more than one column wide, unless the person is the subject of an in-depth profile. Group shots should be used large enough for the faces to be recognizable, with the extraneous parts of the photograph cropped away.

Never use a bad photograph or a poor illustration, no matter what the reason. It will make your journal look shoddy. For the best black and white reproduction you need the best black and white prints or, if necessary, a good-quality colour print.

Production

Typesetting and layout

With the advances in computer technology typesetting and layout can sometimes be done in-house.

At the most basic level, a journal can be produced from word-processed or neatly typed copy running from the top to the bottom of the page.

Desktop publishing (DTP) systems allow the trained operator to place word-processed copy in columns and add headlines of varying sizes, rules, boxes, etc.

They also allow the editor to change the copy, either to fit the space allocated or to update the story, right up until the page layouts go the printers.

The other alternative is to give the copy with a rough page layout to a designer who will have the copy typeset and then produce page layouts for your approval. Most typesetters will convert word-processed files on a floppy disk, which saves time and money.

Reproduction

The main options for reproducing the completed page layouts are photocopying and printing.

Photocopying is quicker but more expensive than printing if more than, say, 300 copies are required. It is probably most suitable for fast-news bulletins that can be photocopied on both sides of an A4 sheet. Pre-printed paper with a masthead can be a cost-effective way of improving the look of the bulletin.

Printing is cheaper per unit for large volumes. Cost can also be minimized by restricting the number of colours. Just two can be used very effectively – black for the body text and photographs and one other colour for the masthead, some headlines, rules and tinted boxes.

If the pages have been laid out on a DTP system, laser-printed pages can be supplied to the printers. For even better quality, a DTP bureau can print pages from the disk direct on to film.

Many DTP systems include a scanner for importing photographs or illustrations direct into the page layout, but better print quality can usually be achieved by asking the printer to drop them in.

Distribution

Without an effective distribution network, even the best journals can languish unread in heaps.

For staff newsletters, a well-targeted internal mail distribution to clinics, wards and departments is often the most effective method. Local 'reporters' can also be responsible for maintaining and monitoring distribution in their areas.

Small, targeted distributions to external audiences are best done by mail or, if you can set up an effective and reliable team, by hand. Community newspapers can be distributed relatively cheaply through health service outlets, such as health centres, clinics, hospitals and out-patient waiting rooms; libraries, citizens' advice bureaux and social centres; and local organizations, such as carers groups, Women's Institutes, retirement groups, and chambers of commerce.

Some community newspapers are aimed at the general public through door-to-door distribution. This can be done with your local free newspaper(s) and the advertising leaflets that accompany it, or by the Post Office. Both methods have to be paid for. When arranging distribution in the community, be aware that free newspaper and advertising networks tend not to reach areas of known poverty and unemployment, which may be areas you particularly want to reach.

Exhibitions and audio-visual aids

The underlying aim in the planning of any exhibition, small or large, simple or complex, is to get a message across to one or more of an organization's audiences as effectively and economically as possible, and with the least amount of time in preparation.

A great deal can be achieved by the careful use of traditional, inexpensive methods and materials. If cost is an important factor, a do-it-yourself approach will often be necessary. If speed or sophistication is vital, it is better to use outside professional help. Whichever course is adopted, it is advisable to:

- use photographs, drawings and maps wherever possible, rather than words

- keep captions and other text short (with any additional information being given in a leaflet)

- ensure lettering is legible

- eliminate anything which is not absolutely vital to the message of the exhibition

- work out the amount of time needed to prepare the exhibition – and double it!

DO-IT-YOURSELF EXHIBITIONS

Most trust hospitals and community services have a mass of photographs, plans, sketches, printed literature and archive items which, properly presented, can make a fascinating exhibition. Even if a do-it-yourself approach might, at first, appear to be unglamorous and unadventurous, it does have advantages:

- The materials are to hand and relatively cheap.

- The format can be regularly and easily changed if new developments take place.

- The display can be put in a corridor or mounted on a wall so that
it takes up little space.

- It can be taken to the audience.

- There is no need for constant supervision as there might be if
expensive visual aids or working models were used.

Display boards and materials

Display boards, on which the display materials (photographs, drawings, text, etc) are mounted, are normally either self-standing, with
permanent fixings along their edges to join one board to the next, or
they clip into light metal frames. The most effective covering is loop-
stitched nylon on to which Velcro-backed exhibits can be mounted.

Another way is to mount items like posters, photographs, plans and
text directly on to display boards, using double-sided adhesive tape or
an adhesive spray. To avoid the exhibits tearing or curling, they can be
mounted on card or lightweight foam board first, again using an adhesive spray.

Lettering and illustrations

These are best done by using a desk top publishing (DTP) system or
word processor and a laser printer. Modern photocopying equipment
can be used to enlarge titles, captions and graphics. Photographs can
be blown up to A4, A3 and even A1 size on many reproduction systems in health service reprographic departments.

Vinyl graphics and computer die-cut lettering from sign makers can
make effective titles and headlines.

Layout

Since an aspect of most do-it-yourself displays is lack of time, as well
as shortage of money, there is not much point in spending hours ago-

nizing over artistic merit. The best thing to do is to keep the display simple and uncluttered, using text and bright colours sparingly.

In the absence of a 'designer's eye' for shape and form, it is best to stick to a simple grid system for the layout (see Figure 4). This will give even the most mundane material a sense of cohesion and style. For a more daring approach, the display boards or panels can be treated as though they are the pages of a magazine. If a magazine page pleases the eye, the same layout several times larger on a board or panel will probably do so, too.

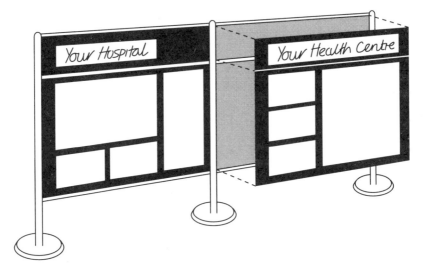

A panel of foam board, with items permanently fixed, can be placed on a display board and easily removed. Doing this and using a layout based on a simple grid helps to ensure that the whole exhibition has the same cohesion and style wherever it is shown.

Figure 4: A do-it-yourself exhibition display

Using three dimensions

There is no need to restrict exhibitions to two dimensions. The introduction of a simple model, for example, will help to change the 'feel' of the whole layout. Photographs and other flat items can be displayed in a three-dimensional way by mounting them on thick material – one-inch deep polystyrene, for example, or foam board – which will hold them proud of the display surface. Combining this technique with the use of strong contrasting colours can produce dramatic effects.

Space permitting, the three-dimensional technique can be taken further. Photographs, drawings or text can be mounted on the faces of large cubes made from foam board. The cubes can be placed by themselves on a table or can be stacked, either according to a pre-planned grid or in a more random fashion.

MAJOR EXHIBITIONS

A do-it-yourself exhibition which suffers from creeping growth may become not so much a major exhibition as a disaster. Larger exhibitions usually call for outside professional services and will need to incorporate most, if not all, of the following:

• large photographs for impact

• typesetting

• imaginative and skilful use of colour

• very big display boards and panels, or a large number of them

• complex models

• surface protection (such as lamination, spray varnishing or clear acrylic sheeting) to avoid damage to the boards or panels

• video or slide-tape machines or special lighting effects.

Specialist services

There are companies throughout the country offering exhibition design and production services. They will write text, obtain photographs and drawings, have them superbly displayed, and deliver the whole exhibition on display panels to the client. This is easy for the client, but can also be expensive.

It is possible to save money simply by knowing what is and what is not possible and by having some idea of the most economical and effective ways of presenting a display – for example, by choosing standard colours rather than insisting on relatively exotic ones.

Mobile exhibitions

A mobile exhibition trailer is a major investment. The following questions need to be considered before making a decision to purchase one:

- What is the mobile display intended to achieve?
- What are the advantages of mobility?
- Can the existing vehicle (say a caravan) be adapted, or will one have to be purpose-built?
- If one can be adapted, will it be large enough?
- Can you provide an adequate entrance and exit and manage the flow of people?
- Can you provide access for people with disabilities?
- Is it to be a mobile office or used simply for storing leaflets and equipment?
- Do fire regulations have to be taken into account?
- Will it be easy to tow and maintain?
- Will an extra member of staff be needed to drive it from venue to venue?
- Are there insurance difficulties?
- How often will it be used?
- How much will it cost?

Exhibition shells

Shells can be hired at large exhibitions. A shell is simply a structure consisting of three walls and an opening which faces on to a corridor or walkway. Display panels are fixed to the walls and a fascia panel is placed above the shell.

Before hiring a shell, the exhibitor should make sure any existing display panels will fit onto the walls, unless new, made-to-measure panels are to be ordered. Leaflet dispensers should be easily accessible, including for people in wheelchairs.

The exhibitor should check what the cost of hiring the shell includes. Does the quoted price include the provision of an electric point for showing slides; additional lights for display panels; a harness or frame for suspending the lights; the hire of furniture; and storage facilities for leaflets and personal belongings?

To get the full value of taking space at a large exhibition, it is worth observing these do's and don'ts:

Do organize the display to encourage people to come on to the stand and look around.

Don't block the entrance with tables, chairs or an abundance of pot plants.

Do give people a chance to read at least some of the display before asking if they would like further information or help; people will probably be reticent about talking as soon as they step on to the stand.

Don't stand intimidatingly at the front of the stand.

Do keep the stand tidy: no empty cups and half-eaten sandwiches, and no ashtrays full of cigarette ends (and, preferably, no ashtrays at all).

Don't keep all printed material piled in cardboard boxes; use leaflet racks which are accessible.

Do keep video or slide-tape sequences short: most people will stand and look for only two or three minutes, and a message has to be put across to them in that time.

AUDIO-VISUAL AIDS

Audio-visual programmes, notably synchronized slide-tape presentations and videos, can be produced in a range of styles, from the simple and cheap to the sophisticated and expensive. Which is used depends on the resources available, the likely audiences, and the context in which they are shown. Audio-visual aids are often used as part of a presentation to illustrate a talk, particularly where an audience of, say, local residents is being encouraged to support a new project in their community, or staff are being introduced to organizational changes.

Synchronized slide-tape

A synchronized slide-tape is a succession of 35 mm colour transparencies, a voice commentary on cassette and a system of putting electronic pulses on the cassette so that it will operate a projector carousel automatically. It is one of the simplest, cheapest and most flexible of all audio-visual aid techniques. But like other techniques, it can be badly done or used for the wrong reasons. A slide-tape package is most effective and useful in the following contexts:

- At the start of a talk or lecture, where a large amount of information needs to be conveyed with accuracy and in a way that will not lose the audience at an early stage. This leaves the speaker free to develop certain themes based on more detailed information already given. It also prevents the audience from getting bored through listening to the same voice and style of delivery for too long.

- In a series of meetings over a period of time, when a particular message or theme needs to be communicated with accuracy and consistency and when it is likely that different speakers will be used on each occasion. Whatever the individual variations of presentation and emphasis, there will always be a core of common material.

- When an automatically operated audio-visual aid is needed in, for example, the reception area of a building. For visitors, it relieves the tedium of waiting and at the same time can convey messages from the organization.

A slide-tape should last no longer than 15 minutes. Anything longer is likely to bore the audience. Some slide-tapes last as little as five minutes but do a very effective job.

An organization planning a slide-tape must decide first what it wants to say to its audience, and what it wants them to think or do after seeing the presentation. The language and style of the slide-tape will be influenced by the likely target audiences.

Assuming it is to be produced in-house, with minimal use of outside resources, the first step is to write the script and visualize the accompanying slides. These tasks should go hand in hand. It is a mistake to write the script first and then to start thinking about the visuals. Commentary and pictures must be complementary and mutually reinforcing, and the impact of succeeding slides as they flash on the screen can affect content of the spoken commentary.

The script and the description of the slides should be written side by side on a sheet of paper, commentary on the left, visual on the right. If this discipline is maintained throughout, voice-over and visuals should mix naturally. Otherwise, there is a risk of an artificial match which will not work.

One of the biggest difficulties with a slide-tape is to maintain a sense of pace and movement. Because the images projected on the screen are flat and immobile – unlike the continuously moving image of a video or film – a slide should not be left on the screen for longer than 10 seconds, and the length of exposure of successive slides should be varied as much as possible. Too long an exposure will prove tedious for the viewer. On the other hand, too many slides passing through too quickly will not give the viewer time to absorb the images properly.

Sentences should be simple and to the point, with only 20 spoken words or so against each visual. Graphics should also be simple because they cannot stay on the screen for long.

Video programmes

The availability of reasonably-priced video cameras and recorders has placed video-making within the reach of everyone. A video presentation can concentrate the minds of an audience and enliven and illuminate an otherwise dull or complex subject.

Video is intimate, like a television set in the living room. It is eminently suitable for reaching small captive audiences – for example, in an antenatal clinic to promote parentcraft classes. In a sensitive issue, such as the development of new homes for people with learning disabilities, it can present the human side of the proposals to help an audience see that the plans are about real people and not about some remote concept.

Because television viewers are a sophisticated audience, the writing, filming and editing of a video must be of a professional standard. If they are not, viewers will mentally switch off.

The message must be as simple and economical as possible. Any temptation to linger on aesthetically pleasing images should be resisted: make them half a second too long and the point could be lost.

As in television documentaries, it is better to go for real-life situations, with real people – patients, doctors and nurses – rather than, say, amateur actors recruited for the purpose. Prepared statements should be avoided, although the participants should be given the chance beforehand to discuss the ground to be covered.

A voice-over commentary is less boring than talking heads, and the use of credits, diagrams and illustrations produced by a graphic designer can add a professional touch to the programme.

Events and meetings

An 'event', whether public meeting, conference, reception, launch, exhibition or ceremonial occasion, must be planned down to the smallest detail if it is to be successful. But three questions have to be answered first:

- Why hold the event at all?

- What do we want to achieve?

- Is it the best way to reach our goal? For example, a leaflet, newsletter or newspaper advertisement will reach many more people than the largest exhibition or public meeting.

Events are useful where they add value to a message. The ceremonial opening of a new health centre or hospital is not necessary in an operational sense. Yet few new developments are commissioned without one. The official opening makes a statement about the place of the new development in the community and the pride that staff, designers and builders take in it. And an exhibition about quality, for example, makes a statement about the importance of the subject far more effectively than a newsletter.

An event – any event – brings people together. The message is conveyed by direct contact and experience and is therefore far more powerful than a message communicated indirectly through the printed word.

But managers thinking of arranging an event need to weigh up the amount of time and effort involved on the one hand and the potential benefits – not least those of winning the audience's interest and commitment – on the other. They need to bear in mind, too, that if the job is to be done thoroughly, one person should be put in charge of all the detailed arrangements. This person will need to give perhaps half their time to it at first. Later, it may become a full-time job until the event is over.

TYPICAL HEALTH SERVICE EVENTS

Among the most common health service events are:

- public meetings – to promote a new idea or development, seek feedback and, if necessary, enable people to vent hostility or fears

- NHS trust annual meetings – to report the year's activity, explain future objectives and answer questions

- receptions – to involve key opinion formers, enlist their support and network informally

- launches – similar to receptions but on a larger scale, often involving formal commitment to a new service or project

- ceremonial occasions – to demonstrate pride in a building or a service, thank key individuals and attract publicity

- conference – to take the initiative on a subject and raise awareness among potentially interested people

- 'fair' type exhibitions – similar to a conference, often demonstrating breadth of expertise; good for sharing experience and good practice, and for giving people the chance to meet and talk informally.

WHERE TO HAVE THE EVENT

The factors in deciding where to have the event are:

- style

- size

- organizational back-up.

Style of event

The setting must be at one with the purpose of the event: should you be in a conference hall or a village hall, in an exhibition space or an open-air market place? It is possible to mount a well planned, high-profile event in a low-profile venue – indeed, the contrast between a basic venue and a professional presentation can increase the impact –

but rarely, if ever, is it possible to get away with an under-organized or low-profile event in a prestigious venue.

Size of event

This should relate to your intended audience. For a public meeting, you may need the largest hall you can find so that no-one feels excluded. For a small reception or an official opening ceremony, you may want an exclusive guest list, in which case it does not matter if other people are unable to get in.

Organizational back-up

The requirements may be simple (power points, for example) or complex (simultaneous translation facilities, syndicate rooms, full registration services and security control). Either way, the needs must be identified and met in good time. If the managers of your chosen venue cannot themselves mount your event, you must bring in or buy the necessary equipment or expertise. This needs planning and booking well in advance.

When selecting your venue, think about:

- access – car parking, public transport, access for people with a disability, separate entrance for organizers or special guests, signposting
- on-site management – availability of telephones and fax machines, secretarial support or security, extra space for syndicate rooms or refreshments, proximity to the main hall. How easy, or not, is it to obtain access before and after the event to set up and take down any 'stage set', display equipment or other materials?
- audio-visual facilities – public address system, availability of overhead or video projection, recording facilities for later publication of event proceedings.

WHEN TO HAVE THE EVENT

There are strategic and tactical elements in fixing a date.

Strategically, you need to know how the event fits into any wider context – national events, its relationship to your overall public relations programme, the need to take an initiative before someone else steals your idea or puts forward an opposing or different view.

Tactically, you need to know that your target audience is able to attend. Don't, for example, fix a reception for MPs at Westminster during a recess. And don't hold a public meeting at the same time as a major sporting fixture or a top-rated television programme (unless your meeting is a mere token one!).

SPEAKERS AND MAIN GUESTS

Most events have speakers or guests-of-honour. They should be booked weeks, perhaps months, ahead and confirmed in time for their names to appear in the advance publicity.

They should be told what is expected of them and agree to it, preferably in writing. You should tell them whether you intend to invite the press and other media. This may affect what they are going to say.

If you have several speakers, it is wise to ask them in advance what their main points will be so as to avoid overlap or conflict on the day. This also helps in preparing the publicity for the event.

The speakers and main guests should be sent copies of all the publicity material.

They should be asked well in advance if they need overhead projection facilities or other audio-visual aids.

Near the time of the event, they should have a full briefing covering such items as joining instructions, confirmation of programme timings and special instructions; an idea of the size and kind of audience expected; and an indication of whether the event is going to be written up for publication.

MEDIA ATTENDANCE

If journalists are invited, they must have proper facilities. For a small event, a simple press table at the front of the room may be enough. For a big event, a press room, equipped with telephones, fax machines, power points (for lap-top word processors, for example), and a quiet area for interviews, will probably be needed.

An information pack, including programme, speakers' biographies, speeches, and background to the event and to the host organization, should be given to each journalist. For large events, someone (preferably a press or public relations officer or, at least, a person with media training) should be allocated full-time to looking after the journalists. A number of information packs should be available to send to journalists unable to attend.

The main speakers and promoters of the event should make themselves available for interviews by the journalists. Depending on the type of event, the best way to achieve this may be by a press conference at a pre-arranged time to suit the media's deadlines.

PUBLICITY

An event with no people is no event at all. Yet of all the arrangements, advance publicity is often given low priority.

A small event, such as a reception for a few dozen people, can be organized by sending personal letters of invitation.

Larger events, and certainly the more complex conferences, meetings or exhibitions, need a range of publicity to succeed. A typical mix would be posters, leaflets and media coverage. Posters should be on display at the venue and at places where your target audience might gather in numbers. For a public meeting, these could include shops, stores, libraries and schools.

Leaflets, perhaps with a tear-off booking slip, should be sent by direct mail to as many of your target audience as possible. For a conference, this could mean a national mail-shot or distribution with a professional journal. For a public meeting, a voluntary group interested in the subject of the meeting might be able to help by organizing house-to-house distribution of notices of the meeting at little or no cost.

The press – professional or lay – may run an article about the event, or it may be preferable to place an advertisement. This would be useful for an NHS trust annual meeting or a meeting arranged as part of a consultation process.

Publicity material must be out in good time – at least two to three months in advance for a conference and up to six months if you are trying to attract exhibitors to an event. The publicity aimed at exhibitors should be separately targeted and run in advance of the general promotion to give them time to prepare.

A month is usually adequate time to organize a public meeting. In a fast-moving situation, three or four days might be enough if posters and newspaper advertising are used effectively. As a general rule it is important to build in enough time to print and distribute publicity material, especially if the event is only a few weeks away.

EVENT MANAGEMENT

A successful event is like a swan on a river: whatever is happening below the surface, the appearance is serene. Your audience must never feel at a loss about what to do or where to go, and the quiet professionalism of the event must be such that they want to stay to absorb your messages.

Whatever the scale of the event, every person who arrives should be met and shown where to go. Registration is the normal way of doing this at larger events. For small-scale ones, an usher at the door is enough.

A programme, brochure or catalogue (depending on the type of event) is useful. This can range from a simple typed and photocopied sheet to a full-colour publication. All large events – and small events in large venues – need clear signposting. The signs should not be hand-written; they may not be clear and they will probably look amateur-ish. Ideally, the signs should be in the style of the rest of the publicity material.

Everyone should be able to see and hear what is going on. If, for example, the event is a trade fair with many different exhibitors, each stand should be clearly labelled on top of the front fascia, and allow space for crowd circulation. If the event is a conference, the top table needs to be clearly in view; it will almost certainly need to be on a stage or dais, with a good microphone and public address facilities. At a ceremonial event (see pages 126–39) everyone should be able to see the focal point of the ceremony.

Every event needs its 'operations room'. This could simply be a side room where the organizers can hold their final briefing as the audience or guests arrive. At the other end of the scale, it could be a suite composed of a speakers' room, conference office (complete with tele-phones, fax machine, word processing facilities and photocopier) and press room.

For events on health service premises, a manager's office is often used as the operations room. In these cases it is wise to dedicate the office solely to the event; the manager will get little or no other work done on the day of the event and should be prepared for this.

STAGED PUBLIC MEETINGS

The advent of NHS trusts, with their obligation to hold annual meet-ings in public, has brought a different dimension to NHS accountability.

The model for the annual meetings is not the gathering in a local hall to hear plans for new developments (or cuts), but much more the annual meeting of a private sector company. NHS trusts which follow the old model risk hostile comments, since such events often serve, by accident or design, as a vehicle for opposition or anger.

This kind of staged meeting (whether by trusts or, indeed, any other health service organization) combines an opportunity to mount a positive, effective presentation with a chance to give feedback to the audience through a question-and-answer session. Elements of such an approach include:

- distribution of information, for example, an annual report to all participants

- a presentation by the chairman, backed by audio-visual aids

- efficient 'front of house' management of the meeting.

It helps the flow of the meeting if questions can be submitted in advance – for example, by completing a slip on arrival and giving it to the person in charge of 'front of house' arrangements. The chairman of the meeting can then ensure that questions are not duplicated and that they go to the right people for a full response. This need not lead to a false or covertly 'managed' meeting. Indeed, if there is any suspicion that difficult questions are being ducked, the audience will soon let the platform know. Done carefully and sympathetically, such handling of the meeting can help focus attention on key messages and help the audience feel that their time has been well spent.

Follow-up questions should be encouraged. These are a useful means of checking that the answer has been understood, and also help to make sure that all important issues are fully aired.

The people who answer the submitted and follow-up questions will be in command of their subject. But inevitably questions are sometimes asked to which no-one can give an immediate reply – perhaps about an individual patient. In that case, the chairman or person who has been asked the question should give an undertaking to answer it in writing as soon as possible and must fulfil the undertaking.

Rehearsal of the meeting is essential: everyone involved must have complete confidence in any audio-visual aids to be used, the venue, the content of the presentations, the style in which they are to be delivered, and the handling of issues most likely to be raised by the audience.

The need for rehearsal is not confined to an NHS trust, of course. Any event that combines a range of speakers or a variety of techniques benefits from a technical rehearsal at the very least.

EVALUATION

Evaluation of an event can be done in various ways. If a registration system has been used, the names and addresses of the people who attended will be available. Some or all of them can be sent a questionnaire or be contacted by telephone or letter for their views. Where registration is impractical or not used (often the case with public meetings or exhibitions) evaluation forms should be given out as people arrive, or placed on seats before the event begins.

In a very few cases, such as a formal ceremony, evaluation in this way is not appropriate. To find out if it really was a success or not, 'soft' evaluation is necessary. Talk to a few of the people who were there (perhaps by telephone a day or two later) and hold a debriefing session for the organizing team, to explore their views and feelings.

EVENT REPORTS

Many events lend themselves to a concise report. For a conference it should be possible to get copies of each speaker's presentation in advance, but you may have no alternative but to tape-record and transcribe the proceedings, and to edit the resulting manuscript. Speakers and the audience should be told if the proceedings are being recorded.

If a report is produced after the event, it must be topical; unless the information is of fundamental importance it may not be relevant or interesting after two or three months.

Someone should be given the job of producing the report and to do so well within this timescale (bearing in mind, though, that production alone can take two or three weeks). If the deadline cannot be met, the value of producing the report should be seriously questioned.

Organizer's checklist

(covering the main requirements for a typical large meeting or conference)

- Fix theme, style, venue, and date.
- Free or paid for?
- If paid for, set up accounts and banking procedures.
- Set budget.
- Identify lead person to manage the administration and give dedicated time and support.
- Devise plan to co-ordinate programme planning, venue and site management, speakers, VIPs, bookings and publicity.
- Book key speakers and VIPs; confirm date and venue.
- Send out advance publicity.
- Set up systems to confirm delegate bookings and general delegate list (if required).
- Develop and confirm detailed programme.
- Send out detailed publicity.
- Confirm detailed arrangements for all participants and send out.
- Set up system for publishing report (if required).
- Send out media publicity.
- Prepare delegate pack and final programme.
- Draw up 'front of house' staff rota.
- Confirm with venue management:
  a) seating
  b) layout plan
  c) power, lighting, public address system, audio-visual requirements, recording arrangements
  d) catering
  e) 'operations room'.
- Check all equipment and facilities are in place as requested, such as:
  a) water and fruit juice for speakers and VIPs
  b) registration facilities
  c) seating or room layout
  d) floral displays
  e) catering
  f) 'front of house' team briefed and ready
  g) 'operations room' ready.

Royal visits and other ceremonial occasions

As with all public events, a ceremonial occasion, such as a visit by a member of the Royal Family or other distinguished person, calls for meticulous planning. No detail should be missed if the occasion is to be successful. Choosing the most appropriate person to invite is itself a step calling for careful judgement.

ROYAL AND MINISTERIAL VISITS

An invitation to a member of the Royal Family should be extended only in the case of a major event, such as the opening of a hospital or of a unit or service in which the individual member has a personal or special interest.

The Royal Family plan their diaries six months in advance. The diary of events for the first six months of the year is normally finalized in November of the year before, and for the last six months, in May of the same year. A letter sent earlier than those dates might receive a reply from the Private Secretary saying the invitation would be considered at the next diary meeting.

It is advisable to contact the Lord Lieutenant as soon as possible. He or she is the Queen's representative in any large town or county. The Lord Lieutenant may wish to extend the invitation on your behalf. If not, his or her office will certainly wish to be kept up-to-date with the arrangements and will provide advice and guidance.

Whether the approach is made by the Lord Lieutenant, a health service chairman, the chairman of a charity or any other person, it is important that it comes from only one person. Private offices of the Royal Family prefer to deal with one contact; this avoids confusion and any possible breakdown in protocol.

If the invitation is accepted, the Private Secretary will want to see an outline programme of the ceremony as soon as possible and a detailed, timed schedule three weeks before the event.

If a member of the Royal Family is not appropriate or cannot attend the event, an invitation may be made to the Secretary of State for Health or one of the health ministers. The invitation should be made by the chairman. The Secretary of State, if unable to attend, will pass the invitation to one of the ministers.

An NHS trust should inform the chairmen of both the district health authority and the regional health authority of the invitation. Trusts, although relatively independent, may consider it good public relations to invite them to the function as distinguished guests.

CONSTRUCTION SITE CEREMONIES

Turf-cutting and topping-out ceremonies – the traditional start and end of construction of any building – technically belong to the domain of the building contractors. In the case of a topping-out, the contractors will lay on refreshments for the entire building force as a 'thank you' for their efforts.

Because they are contractors' events, regional, health authority, trust and unit representatives should be present only by invitation.

Some of the larger contractors like to handle most of the arrangements themselves, including publicity, guest lists and the programme.

But it is important to contact the contractors as soon as possible, not only to give them an idea of the people you would like to be invited, but also to liaise on various arrangements. This is especially important for things like catering and the sound system – items that might be assumed by the organizers as the unit's or health authority's responsibilities and discovered only at the last moment not to be.

CHARITY-FUNDED SCHEMES

New units and equipment for the health service are sometimes provided through fund-raising by charities and local organizations such as Rotary Clubs and Round Tables, or national bodies like the Variety Club of Great Britain or the Cancer Research Campaign.

The formal handing-over of equipment, or the opening of a unit built with the help of privately donated funds, is usually arranged jointly by the organization which has raised the money – and which may wish to gain maximum publicity from any ceremony – and the unit. The question of who has the leading role should be decided early on, particularly if there is more than one charity concerned. The key to this is usually the proportion of the cost of the new unit or piece of equipment.

The charity should certainly have a strong say in how any ceremony is arranged and how its chairman and leading fund raisers play their part in the function. However, the manager of a unit in the NHS should not let this alter the fact that the NHS should be the host on the day. If the charity takes over full control of the function, official protocol may be broken, perhaps with regional, health authority and trust chairmen not knowing about the function until too late, or patients and staff being inconvenienced.

The guest of honour may be an entertainer, sports personality or politician. Sometimes a member of the Royal Family may attend, particularly if the organization has royal patronage or personal contacts with the Royal Family.

The organization will often have its own press office that will do much of the publicity work for the function, but it should liaise with the health service people handling the media arrangements.

THE GUEST LIST

In drawing up a guest list for a visit or other ceremony, always try to cover every angle of the project, paying close attention not only to VIPs, but also to the people who worked on the scheme. People can be hurt if they are missed off the list, even if by accident. This may mar the whole event, not only for the individual but for the organizers because they will be blamed afterwards.

Contractors should be asked for the names of their representatives, but the number should be limited to, say, two people per contractor, particularly if the scheme is a large one with several sub-contractors involved.

Other people to remember may include the medical staff committees, the local authority, the community health council and volunteer groups.

Except in the case of a Royal or ministerial visit, an invitation to the mayor is optional, but, as the community's leading citizen, he or she should always be considered. Others to be considered are local MPs, leagues of friends and interested community groups, and, in the case of a building, the architects, engineers and members of the project team.

A detailed guest list should be sent to the guest of honour as soon as it has been drawn up. It should also be sent to the regional chairman, if involved.

The welcoming and platform or VIP party – those guests who will be in the immediate presence of the guest of honour – should be kept as small as possible. During tours of new projects, large parties should be split into smaller, manageable groups of eight to ten. And there should be a guide for the VIP party and the other groups. The guides should be the people who are most familiar with the scheme.

INVITATION CARDS AND LETTERS

Cards and letters of invitation should be sent to all guests at least a month before the function, or earlier if possible. This gives them time to reply and arrange their diaries.

The card or letter should give, in order:

- the host organization

- the object of the function

- the guest of honour's name

- the unit and its address

- the date and the time of the function, or

- the time guests should gather, and where.

It should end with 'RSVP' and the name and address of the person to whom the reply should be sent.

Once replies have been received, a letter giving more detailed information about the location of the event, how to get there and guidance on car parking may be helpful. Additional information, such as the time they should arrive, should be sent to the guests in the platform or VIP party.

BROCHURES

A brochure can be helpful, not only because of the information it contains but also as a memento of the day.

For major events, the brochure might include a portrait picture of the guest of honour, background details of the object of the function, and a reference to the guest's links with the building or organization.

For the opening of a new building or equipment, the information might include a history of the unit, description of the new building or equipment with photographs or drawings, details of services and facilities, and the names of the commissioning project teams, architects, contractors and fund raisers.

If possible, the brochure should be written and produced in a way that allows it to be used afterwards as an information booklet.

A ROYAL PORTRAIT?

If a photograph of a Royal guest is needed, permission should be sought from the Private Secretary, who will supply a formal portrait or provide the name of the approved photographers who have taken the most recent official portraits.

If a colour portrait is wanted for signing, the photographer should be given at least three weeks to produce the print. Most members of the Royal Family will sign the portrait (normally at the same time as the visitors' book). Some prefer to sign it later and send it back. Others may only sign if they are patrons of the unit or have a very special interest in the work being done. The Private Secretary will clarify the position.

A PLAQUE?

A commemorative plaque is a popular and permanent way of marking a ceremonial occasion. Its unveiling offers a central focus to a function. The decision on whether or not to have a plaque should be made as early as possible because it takes at least a month to have it made. A number of firms specialize in making plaques. A public relations adviser, supplies manager or estates manager should be able to give advice.

The wording for the plaque should contain only basic facts:

- the name of the host organization
- the name of the unit (or just, 'this building')
- the name of the person performing the ceremony
- the date of the ceremony.

The proposed wording should be sent to the guest of honour for approval. With the Royal Family, the intended wording should be sent to the Private Secretary as soon as possible: members of the Royal Family like to give their consent to the wording personally.

Where a charity has taken a leading part in the fund raising, it is usually acceptable to add an expression of gratitude at the bottom of the plaque, but a member of the Royal Family may still prefer that only the basic information is given.

Once the wording has been approved, the following things have to be decided:

- the size and shape of the plaque – square, rectangular or hexagonal
- materials – steel, wood, slate or marble
- colour – dark wording on stainless steel or gold inlaid wording on green slate, etc.

Finally, the position for the plaque has to be chosen. The best place is usually in a central waiting area, reception hall or linking corridor so that, if possible, the main ceremony can take place in front of all the guests.

If the final site of the plaque is somewhere too small for all the guests and the unveiling ceremony is to be a central part of the day, the plaque can be put on a temporary stand or plinth in a bigger area and installed later.

The plaque itself should be fixed so the central line of wording is at eye level for a person of average height.

THE CEREMONY

The order of ceremony normally follows a set pattern, whether the guest of honour is a member of the Royal Family or other distin-guished person.

There are four main stages:

- welcomes and presentations
- the tour
- the ceremony
- refreshments and departure.

Welcomes and presentations

On arrival, the guest of honour is welcomed by the chairman of the host organization (usually a trust or health authority), except in the case of a Royal visitor who is normally welcomed by the Lord Lieutenant or the mayor.

The Secretary of State or a government minister takes precedence over the host chairman. The person taking the lead in welcoming the guest should present the host chairman as soon as possible. The people who will be making up the VIP or Royal party are then presented to the guest by the host chairman.

The guide should be the last person on the welcoming line-up and should join the host chairman in inviting the guest of honour to tour the premises. On Royal visits, the guide should walk slightly ahead of the Royal guest.

The tour

The Royal or VIP party tours the unit. Every opportunity should be made for the guest of honour to meet staff, patients and their relatives. Members of the Royal Family like to talk with doctors and nurses about their work, particularly when it involves advances in treatment. And of course, they enjoy talking with patients and relatives – none of them likes empty clinics or wards.

Members of the Royal Family enjoy talking with patients and relatives. None of them likes empty clinics and wards.

With Royal visits, when there is often a large number of civic dignitaries – the mayor, high sheriff, leader of the council, and so on – it is a good idea to have a civic party either five minutes behind or going on a different route.

It is acceptable to have the tour after the ceremonial opening, particularly if there are difficulties over timings or logistics. But guests of honour, and especially members of the Royal Family, normally prefer to go round a unit or building before they perform the official ceremony.

It is vital to avoid any possibility of the Royal guest mistaking the route. He or she will tend to be at the front of the touring party, with the guide, and with the host and chairman at his or her shoulder. Wrong turnings must be blocked off – by smiling nurses and patients – and fire doors opened by obliging staff. Mistakes can be embarrassing. Women guests of honour have been known to stride into the men's toilets: 'Oh, how very useful'.

The ceremony

The ceremonial – official opening, launch or other ceremony – is the centre-piece of the visit, particularly for guests. For most of them, this is the only time they will be in the guest of honour's presence.

The chairman of the host organization should say a few words of welcome to the guest of honour and everyone else at the event, and then formally invite the guest of honour to perform the ceremony.

The guest of honour performs the ceremony – unveiling a plaque, pulling a switch or turning a turf – and may want to make a speech. A Secretary of State or minister who is the guest of honour will usually want to make a speech. Members of the Royal Family normally speak only when they have a special interest in or patronage of the organization connected with the building.

A vote of thanks follows. It is often given by a senior member of the medical, nursing or paramedical staff. In addition to thanking the guest of honour, he or she should talk briefly about the history and future of the unit. Project teams and major building contractors should also be thanked. If there has been a large charity involvement, the vote of thanks, or an additional word of thanks, may be given by the chairman of the charity, who will also have other people to thank.

Once the expressions of thanks have been completed, a posy or bouquet of flowers and a gift may be presented to the guest of honour. Posies may also be presented to other important guests.

Refreshments and departure

The type of refreshments and the costs incurred depend on the number of guests and on the time of the function. Mid-morning functions normally finish with a buffet lunch or, in some instances, a sit-down meal. Tea and cakes are acceptable at an afternoon function. Whether wine or sherry is served is up to the organizers.

A full sit-down meal is rare. Normally a buffet lunch or afternoon tea will suffice. Tea and cakes at an afternoon function work out cheaper per head than the refreshments of a morning function.

The refreshments stage offers another opportunity for people to meet the guest of honour. Members of the Royal Family prefer this stage to be as informal as possible, with people able to eat, drink and relax. But if food is being served in a buffet form and the Royal guest of honour is not staying to eat, it is advisable to delay the food until the guest has left.

Some members of the Royal Family, particularly the older ones, prefer a small group of guests to have tea with, away from the main body of guests. But most prefer to stand and chat over a cup of tea or a cold drink.

What must be avoided is a queue of people snaking through the room or hall in an attempt to meet the Royal visitor. A way to avoid this is to divide the people meeting the Royal visitor from other guests, either by a row of carefully placed flowers, or by using the shape of the room or hall to advantage; an 'L' shape is perfect.

The guests who are to meet the Royal visitor can then be divided into groups of about six. These groups tend almost to form themselves – project team, fund raisers, chosen staff, contractors, designers, and so on.

The groups should be assigned to numbered tables containing their food and drink. Each group should have a designated leader who, once presented, can present the other group members. Ideally, there should not be more than six groups.

The Royal visitor can move from one group to another, being presented to each group leader in turn, either by the guide or by the chairman.

The advantages of this arrangement are that:

- each of the groups gets three or four minutes (or sometimes more) with the visitor

- the Royal visitor is able to concentrate on talking about a particular subject or aspect of the new unit with each group, rather than chopping and changing to talk to different individuals about different subjects

- the organizers and the Private Secretary can have a reasonably accurate idea of the time that will be taken for refreshments

- the 'snake' of people to be presented is avoided.

This procedure has been successful in many Royal visits. Guests who are not in these groups are usually content because they are still having refreshments in the Royal presence.

The Royal visitor should be offered a drink as he or she arrives in the room or hall where refreshments are being taken. The Private Secretary will advise on what they like to have.

The lady-in-waiting or equerry will make it known when the Royal visitor is about to leave. It is helpful to ask the Royal guest to sign the visitors' book at this stage. It allows all guests to know that she or he is about to leave and, more importantly, allows the main guests who will be saying farewell to gather together, ready to follow the guest of honour out. The VIPs say farewell in the reverse order of the welcoming line-up.

FURTHER ADVICE FOR ROYAL VISITS

Before preparing correspondence, or more particularly if you are approached by a Private Secretary wishing to arrange a Royal visit to your unit, be clear what type of visit it will be – a private visit or a formal one involving public duties. If private, full protocol is not allowed and the visit should be kept as low-key as possible with as few people knowing about it as is practicable. However, a Royal person's intention to make a visit 'informal' does not necessarily mean private but more likely as little fanfare as possible and no formal ceremony or speeches. NHS protocol should be followed and the news media are likely to be interested and attend because the visit will be publicized in the court circular pages of national newspapers.

If one member of the Royal Family turns an invitation down, another Royal person may be reluctant to take it up. If you want to make a second invitation, it should be to a more junior member of the family. The Queen and her immediate family come first, then other relatives. If the Queen is invited and declines, she may recommend another member of the family who can be invited instead.

To avoid an embarrassing snarl-up at the main entrance, the invitation card for most of the guests should state an arrival time that is later than the arrival time of the Royal guest. The guests will then arrive while the Royal party is already on the tour. This ensures they are not trying to get into the unit at the same time as the Royal visitor, and also that they do not have to wait too long for the official ceremony. However, those guests who should be available to welcome the Royal visitor should be asked in an accompanying letter to be in the building 30 minutes before the guest of honour's arrival.

In many places, there will not be enough car parking space for all guests. The members of the welcoming party should ideally have reserved spaces. Other guests should be told of the lack of parking space, possibly in a note at the bottom of the invitation card, advising them to travel by taxi or public transport.

The programme must not be unilaterally changed at the last minute. It provides the reference base for everybody involved in the day: the police, stewards, guests, the news media, and the Royal guest. If some change cannot be avoided, everybody from the Private Secretary to the cloakroom attendant should be informed as soon as possible.

The presentations at each stage of the tour should be kept to a minimum. In a hospital, medical and nursing staff should be spread around the ward or unit to allow the guest of honour the opportunity to stop and talk with them and their patients spontaneously. This also avoids repeated line-ups and handshakes.

Ensure the route for the guest of honour does not interfere with essential parts of the unit, such as a hospital's accident and emergency department or impede emergency services. If clinics or consultants' appointments have to be cancelled, notice should be given well in advance to patients and staff.

The refreshments stage is the most dispensable part of the function. If a Royal guest has to leave on time and for some reason has run late on the other stages, then the refreshments may be cut short – ten minutes instead of the allocated 20, for instance. The people in the presentation groups should be warned beforehand that this might happen; it will avoid any disappointment or resentment later.

The news media

The news media are always interested in Royal visits, and the Royal Family like to be seen carrying out their public duties.

The best way to inform the media is through a news release to the editorial offices at least a week in advance. For small events, a letter to the editors of local newspapers, inviting them to the function and providing some background details, will be enough.

In some parts of the country, where there is close liaison with the Lord Lieutenant, the arrangements for media coverage may be undertaken by the Central Office of Information (COI). This is normally the case for visits involving the Queen, the Duke of Edinburgh, the Prince of Wales, the Princess of Wales, the Queen Mother, the Princess Royal, Princess Margaret and the Duke of York.

These visits are controlled by a rota party pass system. This means that a restricted number of photographers, television crews and reporters from the local, national or international media are allocated rota passes for each individual engagement, with the approval of Buckingham Palace. The rota is strictly controlled, and those who have passes will make words and pictures available to non-rota colleagues. The Buckingham Palace press office will attach a note to each rota pass telling the holder exactly where to attend and who will be briefing them.

For visits by other members of the Royal Family, or when other eminent people are attending a ceremonial occasion, media arrangements are normally left to the health service organization and can be dealt with by, or with the assistance of, its public relations adviser.

Whoever makes the arrangements should make early contact with the police, who may offer a liaison officer. It is sometimes useful to invite journalists to the unit a few days before the visit. They can tour the route and meet the liaison officer and any health service staff who will need to recognize them on the day and whose co-operation may be needed for pictures and interviews.

Members of the Royal Family object to certain pictures being taken − for example during a meal or when having a drink − and the VIP refreshments area is out of bounds to the media. Individual members of the Royal Family may have other dislikes, such as flash equipment going off while they are speaking. Most national press photographers are aware of these restrictions; they have covered many Royal visits and many are known personally to the Royal Family and their advisers.

The reporters and photographers should be fully briefed about the route, where they can and cannot go, and which parts of the visit will provide them with the best stories and pictures. They should be given all the available written material, including the brochure, schedule, order of proceedings and any advance copies of speeches.

The media arrangements need particularly careful planning to ensure that photographers keep one step ahead of a Royal guest and take pictures from the best vantage points without disruption. Service lifts, side doors and alternative corridors usually provide a convenient route for them. Television crews will discuss and agree with the organizers beforehand the positions where they will be able to get the best uninterrupted views.

Reporters often prefer to be a separate group, following on behind the visiting party so that they can interview people who have met and talked with the Royal visitor. This is usually more convenient from everyone's point of view. Each group of media people should be accompanied and assisted by a fully briefed member of staff. The Royal visitor's private detective will discuss and agree the press or rota route when he or she visits a few weeks beforehand to review security arrangements.

A press room should be reserved for the media's use as a base during the visit. It should be secure, either locked or kept under watch, so that cameras, film equipment, cases and coats can be stored safely. Ideally, it should have telephones. If not, there should be at least one telephone nearby. Refreshments should be provided, particularly bearing in mind that the VIP refreshments area is out of bounds to the media.

If a distinguished visitor, such as the Secretary of State, is likely to want to say something significant about health service issues, a few minutes should be set aside for a press conference towards the end of the visit, and a room allocated for it.

Public relations campaigns

A public relations campaign is a planned and sustained effort to communicate information and ideas to a defined target audience. Its purpose may be to:

- offer help or advice

- advertise a service

- influence decision-makers

- secure public support for changes

- simply provide more information on a particular issue.

Before running a campaign, be sure about two things. Firstly, what is the objective of the campaign – what is it trying to do? Indeed, is a campaign the most effective way of tackling the issue? If in doubt, ask health service staff who have been involved in campaigns, with subjects ranging from water fluoridation to staff recruitment. And ask those staff whose job it is to know about the issue. The most successful campaigns have been those that have had clear objectives and the support and co-operation of the people nearest the problem being addressed.

Secondly, who will manage the campaign and to whom is he or she responsible? As with any task, it is important to be clear about who is in charge. Without a campaign manager and a clear line of accountability, it will be extremely difficult to ensure that people know what needs to be done, by whom, and when.

UNDERSTANDING THE ISSUES

A thorough understanding of the relevant issues is essential. Specialists in campaign organization may need to be consulted, as may the users of the service in question. However, there is a wealth of existing data on health affairs which often remains untapped. It is not always easy to access this data but, by discussing plans with colleagues at neighbouring practices, trusts, authorities or at the NHS Executive, relevant sources of information can be identified and research costs kept to a minimum. Research may be hard work, but it is worth the effort: good information comes from perspiration and not inspiration.

Three goals should be kept in mind as the data is analysed:

- identification of a single campaign focus

- establishment of good benchmark information (see pages 142 and 182)

- involvement of those critical to the success of the campaign.

This is not work that can be pursued by a single person. As the project manager's knowledge of the issue increases, it should be possible to identify people who can help. Form a campaign team and encourage others to share in the thinking and planning.

THE CAMPAIGN PLAN

A plan enables the organizers to direct the campaign effectively and ensures that resources are invested suitably. However, thinking should not be too rigid; unforeseen pressures may occur.

The plan should be agreed by the organizers and contain:

- the aim(s)

- specific objectives

- target audience(s)

- clear messages

- the actions or feelings required by or from the target audiences

- the methods, mechanisms and materials to be used to communicate with people

- the resources to be used to bring all this about

- a schedule showing what should be happening and when, and who is responsible for each piece of action.

The plan should be shared with the people who will play a part in making it happen. Any problems and uncertainties should be identified, and solutions agreed.

RESEARCH

Three forms of research and evaluation should, if possible, be built into the campaign: benchmark information, tracking research, and post-campaign research and evaluation.

Benchmark information allows the current state of affairs to be quantified and is the measure against which success or failure can be assessed. Pre-campaign testing of messages and materials, with, perhaps, a representative sample of the target audience, may also be useful.

Tracking research is useful for monitoring progress against targets and testing the effectiveness of the campaign. It will also point to any remedial action that might be necessary, whether in the publicity methods being used, the level of resources being invested, or even the messages being communicated.

Post-campaign research and evaluation will allow conclusions to be drawn about the project's effectiveness. It will also identify lessons that can be learned and possibly highlight issues that may need to be dealt with in the future.

USING THE EXPERTS

The organizers must decide what specialist advice and support are needed and how the cost can be met. There are three areas where this applies particularly: copywriting and creative skills, the purchasing of publicity and advertising space (media and print buying), and research.

Campaign materials should appeal to the target audience, use words and pictures that mean something to them, and be placed in areas that give maximum impact. The 'what' and 'how' of the campaign messages, and 'who' says them, need to be rooted in an understanding of the audience's lifestyles and interests.

For media and print buying advertising agencies have access to data on the habits and motivations of the public and the relative merits of different media.

Research findings, if they are to be useful, should be based on accurate information, be compiled from relevant sources and samples, and draw firm conclusions only when there is sufficient evidence.

COMMUNICATION

Everyone involved in the running of the campaign must keep in contact with each other. A successful campaign will generate regular media attention and enquiries from the target audience. The messages they receive need to be consistent, and the campaigners must know at all times what is going on and what is being said. Lines of communication must be planned, clear and two-way.

LOCAL VERSUS NATIONAL CAMPAIGNS

High-impact, high-cost nationwide campaigns are not always the best. What applies in one part of the country is not necessarily the case in another. Locally organized campaigns have many strengths. They can be targeted more precisely and respond more rapidly to changing local circumstances. They also benefit from greater ownership and commitment. Indeed, local people may soon be running tailor-made neighbourhood campaigns, with the support of local health organizations.

BUT THERE'S NO PLEASING SOME PEOPLE!

It will not be possible to please everyone. People may disagree with the campaign itself or the approach being taken. This is inevitable. And things will go wrong. But by ensuring that there is good reason to have the campaign, that it has sound objectives and is adequately planned and supported, the chance of failure is reduced to a minimum.

Campaign checklist

• Be clear about the need for the campaign.

• Ensure that everyone is agreed that this is the best approach.

• Appoint a campaign manager.

• Establish lines of accountability.

• Decide on a single campaign focus.

• Obtain benchmark data.

• Secure the commitment of the people involved.

• Agree aim(s).

• Agree specific, quantifiable objectives.

• Identify target audience(s).

• Agree campaign messages.

• Obtain access to the skills needed.

• Define and secure resources.

• Develop campaign methods, mechanisms and materials.

• Devise and work to a campaign schedule.

• Organize lines of communication and keep them open.

• Put in place, and listen to, tracking research.

• Do post-project evaluation.

THREE CAMPAIGNS

Three typical health service campaigns are described overleaf. The first was to guide drug users to appropriate help services; the second was to transfer people from a well-known psychiatric hospital into the community and close the hospital; and the third was to implement a no-smoking policy for an NHS trust's staff, patients and visitors.

Drugs-help campaign

A campaign by Wessex Regional Health Authority (now part of the South and West Region of the NHS) was devised to guide drug misusers towards support services. It was aimed particularly at people using Ecstasy, LSD and amphetamines. The campaign was financed by the Department of Health. The Department wanted to counter publicity that, inadvertently or purposely, had promoted the use of the drugs as an exciting and harmless pleasure.

A campaign team was formed, headed by a campaign manager. It sought guidance from specialists in drugs misuse on the extent and nature of the problem in Wessex. They said that large amounts of Ecstasy were being used and that increasing numbers of people were beginning to have health problems as a result. They believed serious consequences were imminent, that warnings were needed, and that Wessex Regional Health Authority should publicize services that could help. The benchmark information pointed to the need to concentrate on people involved in the 'dance scene', targeting messages at young people aged between 12 and 20 years.

The campaigners agreed on making dance scene drugs the single campaign focus and on the following campaign objectives:

- to raise awareness of the dangers of drug misuse

- to raise the profile of drug agencies which could provide advice, support and counselling

- to provide literature and support material

- to ensure that the campaign was evaluated.

They decided to aim messages at people already taking drugs rather than mount a prevention campaign. Because the group being targeted tended to ignore traditional advertising methods, such as newspapers, messages had to be pitched correctly.

In conjunction with *Help for Health*, a charitable trust which provides information to the public on health matters, the project team ran an 0800 (free) telephone service to provide a focus for advertising. Callers would learn more about the campaign and be put in touch with their most appropriate local service.

With the creative, copywriting and media buying experience of a leading national advertising agency, the team produced and placed printed material to point people to the 0800 number. The material featured an identifiable campaign logo and used fluorescent inks and 'street' terms such as 'acid' and 'speed'. It included posters on billboard sites and the sides of buses, and advertisements in local newspapers and on local radio.

A4 posters and a leaflet, specially designed to interest young people and distributed through drug agencies, explained the hazards and symptoms of drug misuse. Support material for professionals included a 'drugs response manual' giving clear, authoritative information.

The team secured the involvement of the local news media and organized a high-profile media launch for the campaign, involving a health minister. Back-up materials and news releases were produced before, during and after the campaign giving information to the media on its progress.

An analysis of the calls made to the freephone service allowed the project team to track the campaign's effects. The line was confidential, but callers gave their age, said where they had learned about the freephone number, and gave other information that was useful in gauging reactions.

From analysis of this information, the team could track progress regularly – almost by the hour if required. It was clear the advertising was proving effective as the line was receiving up to 70 calls a day in response to the publicity.

The information gathered through the freephone service also proved valuable to the researchers evaluating the project. Findings showed that most people who contacted the freephone service were attracted by one of the posters, particularly those on the sides of buses. Young people praised the artwork and copy. Some found it hard to believe that an organization like a regional health authority of the NHS would be so open about a problem and use everyday language. They also praised the fact that information concentrated on problems and services and did not preach about dangers. That gave the health authority and the campaign credibility among the target audience. This respect for the campaign organizers gave credence to the messages.

Changes to mental health services

Friern Hospital had been providing acute and long-stay psychiatric services in north London for 142 years. North East Thames Regional Health Authority (now part of North Thames Region) planned to close it in March 1993 after a 10-year programme of developing replacement services.

The aims of the public relations campaign associated with the closure were to:

- co-ordinate the communications work of the regional health authority, five health authorities, Friern Hospital, five health service providers and a research team on the closure of the hospital and the development of community based services

- promote understanding of community care among the general public, opinion formers, users and staff, to assist in its successful implementation.

They had to help the public understand why the closure was good news, especially when people saw homeless mentally ill men and women wandering the streets, and explain why moving services from the hospital would not affect crisis intervention services. More than £50 million was being spent on 78 schemes for homes in the community to accommodate the Friern residents.

A communications adviser was appointed by the regional health authority to devise a nine-month work programme. Top priority was given to production of briefing material that could be used for opinion formers such as local MPs, community health councils, councillors and local news media.

The health authorities, provider organizations and Friern Hospital managers fielded a steady stream of media enquiries and wrote to the letters pages of local newspapers.

Research by the Team for the Assessment of Psychiatric Services (TAPS) showed that people transferring from Friern Hospital into the community preferred to move rather than stay, and this was publicized. Managers and various other advocates of community care were groomed in media and public relations skills to promote understanding of the benefits of the changes.

The campaign consisted of three main projects, described below.

Project 1: The briefing

Leaving Friern, Coming Home, a 56-page guide to the changes, involved co-ordinating 15 contributors (*and* getting them to agree with each other's wording on mental health) and gathering information about the 78 schemes to replace Friern Hospital's services. It was launched to an audience of five community health councils in the areas of the new services; their understanding and support were crucially important.

Copies of the guide and individualized letters went to:

- community and voluntary groups

- users and care groups

- purchasers and providers

- local authorities and their social services and planning departments

- family health services authorities

- GP fundholders

- trades unions

- pressure groups

- professional bodies

- mental health organizations

- the NHS Management Executive and Department of Health

- other regional health authorities

- districts in the region with long-stay institutions.

The chairman of Hampstead Health Authority wrote individually to MPs, offering to meet them; many took up the offer.

Project 2: Marking the closure

Many people in north London, while convinced about the development of services in the community, were sad about the closing of Friern Hospital. To focus feelings of loss and ease the transition in a managed way, events were held that included:

- *The Friern Hospital Exhibition, 1851 to 1993*, using the hospital's own art boards and without professional design so as to minimize costs.

- A multi-denominational service of thanksgiving, attended by 500 people, and with nurse managers, most of whom had trained and worked at Friern, enthusing about long-stay patients having their own bedrooms in homes they could at last call their own in the community.

- A commemorative booklet, with patients and staff involved in the writing and production so that it became 'their' booklet.

Project 3: Training sessions in dealing with the media and handling crises

These were run by communications consultants for managers and spokespersons from local and regional health authorities and providers. The training gave them confidence to handle the antici-pated upsurge in interest in the lead-up to the closure. A question-and-answer pack was produced.

The main successes from the overall programme were:

- no problems with opinion formers, no local outcry or opposition, and no negative media coverage

- positive media coverage, and acceptance of the need for change by agencies and the public throughout the districts affected

- commissioning of projects to establish good communications between the new services and the public, together with projects aimed at patients and staff

- interest by other health authorities and providers in the region in the communications aspects of replacement of services and how they fit alongside other aspects, such as personnel, estates and ser-vice development.

No-smoking policy

South Downs Health NHS Trust provides community and mental health services for the Brighton, Hove and Lewes areas in Sussex. One of the trust board's earliest commitments was to introduce a no-smoking policy for all staff and visitors and most patients.

The board agreed that the only exceptions would be: where trust premises were effectively the patient's home; on the rare occasions when a doctor gave permission for a patient to smoke; and in the case of some psychiatric patients who were given designated smoking areas.

The trust recognized that a comprehensive smoking ban would be difficult for some staff who would find it hard to stop smoking while at work. Some patients and visitors were also expected to make life difficult for staff who would have to enforce the ban.

The campaign was launched by the Secretary of State for Health, Virginia Bottomley, and included:

- an information package, containing leaflets for staff, patients and visitors, and posters and stickers

- training for managers and staff in how to implement the policy in sensitive and effective ways

- help (mostly free of charge) for staff who wanted to give up smoking, including stop-smoking groups, counselling, provision of a nicotine replacement, hypnotherapy sessions and acupuncture

- media publicity in the weeks before the campaign start date.

The literature was written by the press and public relations manager in consultation with other senior managers. The leaflets for patients and visitors were placed in reception areas in hospitals and clinics and sent with admission and out-patient appointment letters. The staff leaflet was distributed with pay packets and posters were displayed prominently in all the trust's locations.

The campaign received widespread publicity, locally and nationally, because at the time South Downs Health was going further than many other health service organizations in banning smoking. The provision of clear and sensitively written literature was seen by managers and staff as a crucial lever in implementing the policy successfully.

Health promotion programmes

The promotion of health relies partly on a range of public relations techniques – whether at the highest level in attempting to influence government on tobacco-growing subsidies or at the most local level where someone at a health fair dresses as a carrot and gets people to think about their eating habits.

CAMPAIGNS FOR HEALTH

The Health Education Authority (HEA) runs special campaigns at particular times of the year to promote messages on such major topics as smoking, diet, HIV and AIDS, and alcohol consumption. Each campaign is organized around a day, week or month of activities.

The HEA often provides resource packs for health service organizations taking part. Typical contents would be information on the aims of the campaign, articles for use in the press and in-house journals, camera-ready artwork, posters, leaflets, and stickers. It also suggests activities and gives advice on public relations action, such as writing press releases and organizing photograph opportunities for the media.

This can be augmented by ideas and materials developed with local health service public relations practitioners or advisers. They can help health service managers to make the most of the national materials and to angle stories and give variations on a national theme in ways that appeal to local news media.

LOCAL CAMPAIGNS

Local campaigns which do not have the back-up of national material provide the chance for a lot of creative thinking.

Basic materials can be used to make photograph opportunities for the media withou: calling in celebrities. For example, a health worker can dress up as a carrot or apple to encourage healthy eating, or as a cigarette carton 'kicked' out of a public place on 'no-smoking day'. Costumes can be hired from a fancy dress shop or, if you are creative, made from inexpensive materials.

The secret of a local campaign is the same as for all other publicity events: be original and, if you want a photograph in the local newspaper, think visually.

DIRECT COMMUNICATION

The main channels for giving information in campaigns are the news media, but face-to-face communication with the public is also vital. Opportunities include courses on personal health and fitness and events such as health fairs.

The best results come through interaction with the public. Exhibitors who stand behind a mountain of leaflets, blocking the view of the display, will find that most passers-by do just that – pass by. Health and lifestyle messages are best communicated if people are involved, encouraged to make choices, and helped to recognize the likely effects of those choices on their health.

Communicating choice

Informed choice was a major theme of the *Bodyworld* exhibition, run by Northern Regional Health Authority (now part of Northern and Yorkshire Region) at the 1990 Gateshead Garden Festival. Every visitor to *Bodyworld* went through a lifestyle maze and made choices about diet, smoking, exercise and alcohol. The result of their decision determined how pleasant the next stage of their journey was to be.

continued

Communicating choice (continued)

Bodyworld featured a fairground attraction where visitors were asked to make lifestyle choices that determined if they won or lost in the traditional fairground games. Another feature was an interactive video game, aimed at young adults, which took them through a night out with their friends; they had to make choices about their lifestyle in different situations.

The situations in which visitors found themselves were presented as entertaining games, but the choices they had to make were real and designed to help them think about their own health needs.

Bodyworld had a fitness testing area where visitors could obtain an indication of their present level of fitness and ways they could maintain or improve it. And it provided an area where local health service organizations and other groups had exhibitions to inform people about services and particular health issues.

ON A SMALL BUDGET

1 Interaction

The techniques used at *Bodyworld* (see boxed text above) can be used successfully on a much more modest scale. Interaction is the key.

Quizzes

Where quizzes relate to a display, they can be used to encourage participants (as they thus become, instead of observers) to study the display in order to find the answers. Two aims are achieved: the people will have read the messages and they will have used the information to make choices. At the same time, people staffing the display have the chance to talk with the participants about any difficulty they may have in finding the answers, how they feel about the subject matter, whether they are interested in obtaining more information, and so on.

The quiz sheets can also provide 'quick and dirty' data on people's knowledge of the subject: Did they understand the messages in the display? Are they planning to change their lifestyle? More general questions can be inserted in the quiz, such as: Where and how do you receive most of your information about health?

Games of skill

These help people to remember basic messages through the use of visual metaphors. A popular game is the traditional 'Aunt Sally', in which contestants try to knock over a wooden dolly with sticks or balls. In a health game, the dolly can instead be a target to represent the message you want to convey. It could, for instance, be a wooden representation of a bottle of wine with the number of units of alcohol it contains written on the label. Using tennis balls, the contestant tries to knock over the number of targets that add up to the number of units an individual can safely consume in a week.

The passer-by is drawn into the spectacle. It is fun. Apart from having a good aim, contestants have to gain a certain amount of information to succeed. And, most importantly, they and the people watching are more likely to remember the information.

There are many variations on ideas like these, but the principles are the same:

- The messages should be simple.

- Follow-up information complementing the themes in the game should be offered.

- Displays should be simple. A passer-by needs to be able to see what the display is about without having to read a lot of text or peer past you and a table of leaflets.

- If you want to get a message across to individuals, get them involved. Make it interactive, an experience, something to talk about with family and friends.

- Leaflets, while not everything, can help to reinforce points and provide useful information, such as telephone numbers.

- Good design will give a good idea much more impact.

2 Displays

Displays on portable boards or permanent notice boards are often used in health promotion campaigns. They should be kept simple. It is a mistake to cram a lot of written information on to a display; more information can be given in supporting leaflets.

A display should be like a good advertising hoarding: it should attract and engage attention. It should also be clear what the subject is, what the message is, and who the messenger is.

Materials provided for a national or international campaign, such as World AIDS Day, can be enhanced not only by the way they are used but by adding a few inexpensive extras. In recent years, the symbol of World AIDS Day activities has been a red ribbon, worn to signify support for people who are HIV positive or have AIDS.

A typical display might include a selection of posters produced for the day and others more generally available, plus some balloons. The universal poster with the central theme or visual image can be placed as part of a block of four or more in a square, or any other shape. A giant red ribbon can be draped over the display boards. The central image can be enlarged by a photographer or on a photocopier to produce a giant image, central to the display.

MULTI-AGENCY WORKING

Better health involves individuals in making positive choices for themselves about their lifestyles. However, many factors affecting people's health care are not completely within their control. Health is affected by inequalities associated with poverty, ethnic group, gender and geographical location.

This has given health promotion a community focus that takes in:

- local government
- environmental health services
- public health medicine
- education authorities
- GPs
- health visitors
- health promotion officers
- politicians
- water companies

- highway authorities

- housing associations

- voluntary groups.

All these organizations and individuals need to communicate effectively with each other to make progress on complex issues. Health promotion can often be the catalyst for collaborative ventures, such as devising a policy to reduce accidents among children, which needs the input and action of many groups.

Public relations practitioners and health service managers or staff with public relations responsibilities need to have strong links with these groups to communicate information and the results of the activities to a wider audience – work that needs to be built into health promotion programmes from the start.

7

Choosing the specialists

The main specialists needed by health service managers in their communications work are usually public relations practitioners and graphic designers and printers. Making a decision about whether to employ practitioners in-house or buy them in means considering a range of options.

This chapter examines the options and describes how to set about appointing public relations consultants. It also looks in detail at how to identify good graphic designers and establish productive working relationships with them, and goes through the different stages of preparing, producing and distributing a leaflet or brochure.

Public relations

A health service organization needing public relations support has five options:

1. Give responsibility for public relations work to a member of the staff who is not a public relations practitioner.

2. Employ a public relations practitioner.

3. Appoint an external public relations consultancy.

4. Work with a freelance public relations practitioner.

5. Use any combination of the above.

It then has to weigh the advantages and disadvantages of each option in light of the public relations needs of the organization. Assessing the needs requires a critical approach.

It has to take a hard look at its communications problems and where they are rooted – in, for example, poor relations with the local media, staff or other organizations, or in widespread lack of knowledge about its role, activities and plans. A public relations practitioner in the health service or an external consultant will help the organization to diagnose the problems – confusion about change, lack of dialogue, inadequate information systems, poor training, inter-departmental stresses – and to decide what should be done.

THE OPTIONS

Having done the diagnostic work, the organization should then consider the options.

Give responsibility for public relations work to a member of the staff who is not a public relations practitioner

The advantage of this approach is that the person is likely to have credibility inside the organization and knowledge of its people, issues and plans. He or she can get started quickly. The expense of the new role can be limited to top-up costs instead of the allocation of completely new budgets.

A disadvantage will be the person's lack of specialist skill or knowledge and the need for training. Even with training, the learning curve will be a steep one. Lack of previous experience may make it difficult to establish confidence with local journalists and among colleagues in the organization who will expect their public relations officer to perform magic with the media and any troublesome pressure groups.

Public relations officers are expected to perform magic.

Employ a public relations practitioner

Employing an experienced public relations person means the organization will have someone who soon gets to know and understand what is going on, is a readily available and reliable source of support, can act as a constructively critical 'professional layperson' in the organization, and should be able quickly to establish good relations with the staff, with the media and with other organizations.

However, hiring someone who is experienced may be expensive in salary and overheads. The successful in-house specialist may also need staff to build on the success. Other departments, especially those having to make economies, may resent investment in 'those press people'.

Appoint an external public relations consultancy

A consultancy can bring objectivity and a fresh approach to many of an organization's communications difficulties. The consultancy will employ, or have access to, a range of public relations skills that no single in-house service could afford. Some of these can be used for 'hands-on' support as and when needed, perhaps to complement in-house services in a crisis or emergency.

A health service organization needs to distinguish between the consultancies with health service experience (such as NHS regional press and public relations departments which have now gone independent) and those unfamiliar with the structure and culture of the health service and its complicated networks of professional and managerial relationships. A consultancy without those insights may find it difficult to handle reactive or crisis public relations work and to make early headway, but it may bring in fresh ideas.

Work with a freelance public relations practitioner

Freelances, who may be journalists with additional public relations skills or former health service public relations specialists who became self-employed after the contraction of regional health authorities, can be useful for individual projects, for advice, for devising public relations plans, or for dealing with a specific problem. They can use their knowledge and experience to obtain and, if necessary, manage services such as design, print and photography.

The disadvantage is that the freelance working alone may not always be available when wanted and, in the absence of consultancy back-up, may need to arrange temporary support that is not satisfactory to the client.

Use any combination of the above

The organization can recruit public relations services according to its various needs. For example, an external consultancy might be engaged to work mainly with the board or part of the organization, or to work alongside the in-house specialist(s) to augment their services on a short- or medium-term basis.

This pick-and-mix approach can be erratic and also undermining for the in-house people unless the services are commissioned as part of a coherent public relations strategy.

HIRING PUBLIC RELATIONS CONSULTANTS

Public relations consultants may be large or medium-sized organizations, or individuals with a network of associates specializing in different skills. The health service organization looking for help has to assess what and how much support it needs and to go through the following steps:

- deciding the type of consultancy
- short-listing
- presentation of credentials
- the brief and presentation of proposals
- making the appointment: the contract and fee arrangements
- the programme: monitoring and evaluating progress.

Deciding the type of consultancy

Public relations consultancies range from sole practitioners to large international agencies. In deciding what type of consultancy is required, the organization has to consider whether it wants a small specialist consultancy or a large wide-ranging one. It then needs to ask if the consultancies it has identified:

- have knowledge and experience of health services and of the way they are organized
- possess, or have access to, a full range of public relations skills

- would be employed for advice (in, for example, drawing up a public relations strategy to be implemented in-house) or for both advice and implementation.

Short-listing

A short-list should be drawn up, taking account of:

- relevant experience and capacity to provide the service or support needed

- the opinions of other health service organizations which have used them or dealt with them as journalists or as suppliers (graphic designers or lobbyists, for example)

- 'gut instinct' about the people in the consultancy and how easy or not-so-easy it will be to work with them

- whether they are members of the Institute of Public Relations

- their fees and what these normally include and do not include.

Presentation of credentials

Each short-listed consultancy should be invited to present its credentials to the chief executive or deputy – and, where employed, the in-house public relations or communications manager – to satisfy them that it:

- is financially viable

- has the expertise and the people needed

- has a good track record

- is prepared for enquiries to be made among existing clients.

The perception and insight with which the representatives of the consultancy respond to questions provide other indicators. Mystique and jargon on their part should be challenged.

This is the stage at which to discuss possible financial arrangements – monthly or daily rates, out-of-hours and on-call charges and expenses. It is also the stage at which the organization decides that it can work, or not, with any one of the consultancies (and when each consultancy decides whether it can work with the organization). The next stage is for the organization to prepare a brief, and invite its chosen candidates to present proposals on the basis of the brief.

The brief and presentation of proposals

The brief should set out the type of public relations programme (one-off or longer-term), give background information, and state the level of service or support needed, objectives, budgets (if any) and specific responsibilities. This will help the consultancy price and assign time appropriately when drafting its proposals. A vaguely defined brief will result in an unclear programme and unsuccessful implementation.

Each consultancy should be invited to make a presentation to a high-level panel that should, ideally, include the chairman and chief executive who thus demonstrate their commitment to the chosen programme and to financial investment in it. If possible, it should include someone – perhaps a non-executive member of the board – who has first-hand experience and understanding of public relations services.

Enough time (say 45 minutes) should be allocated to give the consultants a fair opportunity to present their proposals (10–15 minutes) and answer questions. The questions should follow a broadly similar pattern so that comparisons can be made.

Making the appointment: the contract and fee arrangements

Once a decision has been made, the selected consultancy should set out the contractual and fee arrangements so that there is a clear understanding of expectations and requirements from the beginning.

The programme: monitoring and evaluating progress

It may be useful to have a 'trial' period of, say, six months, with monthly reviews of action, progress and plans. A senior manager should be responsible for liaison with the consultancy, for monitoring and evaluating progress, and reporting to the board.

Graphic design and print

Graphic design has a job to do – a job that goes far beyond making something look attractive. A train timetable, for instance, must list all the train times, and it must be easy to use. This will affect the layout, typography and colour.

A classic example of graphic design that does its job *and* looks good is the London Underground map. Graphic design in the health service should be no less attractive and no less functional.

Three obvious factors affecting design are size, weight, and readability. Will the timetable fit into the pocket and the literature dispenser? Will the hospital leaflet and its envelope be inside the weight for second-class postage? Is the text large enough for older people who might be reading it?

The graphic designer will help a client to identify and prioritize key objectives. But often he or she will also assess real need. Called in by a client who 'wants a brochure', the designer may advise that a more effective solution might be a series of letters, a poster or a video.

Having identified and clarified the objectives, the next task is to choose the most appropriate methods to achieve them, and then construct a programme to implement them efficiently.

The skills of graphic designers are widely used to ensure that organizations' corporate messages are accurately communicated to staff, customers and the world at large through such items as corporate identities, annual reports, promotional literature, manuals, instructions, signs, training aids, and so on. This is especially true of the service sector, including the health service.

WHAT CAN DESIGN ACHIEVE?

Good graphic design can help to:

- improve communications
- focus on the individual
- set the climate for change
- challenge the 'ways we have always done things'
- save money.

Improving communications

At its simplest level, good design can communicate facts simply and efficiently, whether the facts are information for patients, data and charts, or signs and warnings. Good design can also communicate ideas. An organization's philosophies and business strategies often achieve concrete expression only in printed literature. Visual style, approach and application can often make more powerful statements about the organization than words can.

Focusing on the individual

Graphic design is interested primarily in the 'user' of the product – the person receiving the visual message. The client and the designer should have the user at the centre of their thinking and safeguard against material focused primarily on the organization. Certainly, the designer, coming from outside the organization, will start from the potential recipient's viewpoint, demonstrating one of the strengths of design: putting the user first.

Setting the climate for change

The material designed and produced for a client may be the first physical expression of abstract ideas. Annual reports, policy documents, corporate identities and other corporate communications exercises present excellent opportunities for reflecting and promoting new ways of working and can themselves encourage changes of attitude inside and outside an organization.

Challenging the 'way we have always done things'

Another benefit of a graphic designer lies in part of any consultant's stock-in-trade-detached, objective thinking. Systems may have been in operation for years. Documents may have existed in a particular form without their effectiveness (let alone their need) ever having been questioned. Embarking on a major design project, particularly to change an organization's corporate identity, presents the chance to rationalize, streamline and review organizational values, not simply of the documentation, but of the systems themselves.

Saving money

Allowing designers to take an overview of needs, and making cost efficiency a part of the brief, can result in savings in production, purchasing and inventory.

GOOD RELATIONS

Graphic designers, although they are in the communications business, are sometimes poor at communicating their functions and benefits. They may not take time to explain to a customer exactly how they work, what to expect, and the basis for charging.

They may assume the client understands the design process when in fact, many people are in the dark about it, partly because design consultants often cloak the subject in mystery. They may use jargon. And they may accept the client's instructions without telling him or her of the consequences or of possible other ways of approaching the job.

A good design consultant will not only encourage the client to consider alternative solutions, but will advise on the cost and time implications. Once they are understood by the client and agreed, the good designer will confirm the instructions.

Designers charge by the hour or day, in much the same way solicitors or accountants do. It is important to remember that for them – and thus for you – their time costs money, whether they are working creatively, travelling, sitting in meetings, researching, briefing printers or trying to read handwritten copy. If your designer has to sit in unnecessarily long meetings, or you supply him with incomplete material, the lost or wasted time must be made up. In a fixed-price contract, it will be the creative input that suffers.

Another obstacle to a good relationship with the designer may be the competitive tendering system. This is essential in the public sector, and has become stricter in the health service in recent years. It has to be recognized, though, that to reap the maximum benefits from partnership with design consultants, a long-term relationship should be established in which the consultant develops a thorough understanding of the client and his or her organization.

A designer will often be willing to invest a lot of time on a client's behalf, developing a personal relationship, learning about the organization, researching and becoming familiar with its operation, marketplace and culture. This will enable him or her to work more effectively, satisfy the client's needs, and thus secure continuing business.

Faced with a system that says, 'No matter how well you do, any future work will be awarded on a basis of price alone', the designer's priority may well be to ensure that he or she makes enough money from the job in hand and avoids 'over-servicing' the client.

GETTING THE BEST FROM DESIGN AND DESIGNERS

This is achieved by:

- choosing well
- building a relationship
- briefing well
- trying to be honest about budgets
- insisting on documentation
- using the advice.

Choose well

Recommendation is always a good start. Then arrange a meeting with the designer. Look at the work of the designer and decide if you are comfortable with it. Find out about the way the designer works and see if his or her approach seems sound.

Enquire about the areas the designer specializes in, particularly if you have a project in mind. These may not always be clear from the portfolio. And, of course, ask about charging. Daily or hourly rates should be only a guideline. A consultancy with experienced staff and a substantial investment in new technology will get a lot more productive work out of a day than a consultancy with just a handful of juniors.

An important ingredient is 'chemistry'. Can you communicate with the consultant and can you see him or her working well with you and your colleagues? If not, the relationship will probably fail, regardless of the quality of work.

If you have the time, or if you are placing an important project, visit the designer's studio or consultancy.

Bear in mind that the size of studio or consultancy is not always a good guide. Many talented designers work alone or in partnership. Low overheads mean they can often do excellent work cost-effectively. However, they may lack the resources for large or complex projects and access to a wider range of specialist experience and expertise in-house. Many overcome this, with varying degrees of success, by working as part of a loose-knit team of associates.

If you are unsure which consultancy to choose and have a sufficient range of work, a good idea is to select a small group of suppliers of varying size and specializations and to use them on a 'horses for courses' basis – the small one-man band for the less complex, cost-sensitive projects, and larger design groups where greater sophistication or resources are required.

Build a relationship

If you are happy with your designers' work, let them know. Provided they continue to do good work and remain cost-effective, carry on using them, subject to the tendering process. The more they learn about your organization, the more the effectiveness of their contribution will grow.

There will probably come a time, however, when the client and the designer outlive each other, particularly as organizations change, as inevitably they do. The moment is usually recognized by both. The separation should be an honest and open one. If it is, the designer will sometimes be able to recommend another person to compete for the work; and the client may be able to suggest new openings for the designer.

Brief well

Discuss your needs with the designer and jointly agree and write the brief. Ask the designer to confirm it. Although the form it takes may vary, it will usually include such headings as:

- background
- objectives
- audience(s)
- constraints
- requirements
- timing
- budgets.

The brief should be used as your benchmark to judge the presented solution.

Try to be honest about budgets

Be honest with the designer about budgets. Most designers would far prefer clients to indicate roughly what they can afford. There have been instances where designers have been asked to quote on a straightforward project in half-a-dozen or more different formats. The clients were looking for the format that came closest to the budget figure. They would have been better off being open with the designers and allowing them to use their expertise to make the most of the money available.

Insist on documentation

As well as confirmation of the brief, insist on documents which detail the instructions given to the designer. If any instruction will result in a change to the original brief or to any cost or time estimate, it should be confirmed in writing first. This practice will avoid any unpleasant post-mortems afterwards.

Use the advice – you are paying for it

Most designers have studied at least four years for their degree and have spent the rest of their working lives developing these skills. The client who pays for their advice and then overrides their decisions, making subjective judgements and changes, is buying a shell of a service.

PRODUCING A LEAFLET OR BROCHURE

The style and format of a leaflet or brochure depend on the content and importance of the message and on the audience at whom the message is aimed. For example, a handbill announcing the staff social club annual general meeting will be a much simpler affair than the director of public health's annual report. You have to consider whether to place the work with a graphic designer and printer or whether it can be done in-house (see page 171 on Production).

Writing and illustrations

When writing a leaflet or brochure for public consumption, try to:

- use short words and sentences
- avoid jargon
- assume a lack of knowledge by the reader about the subject
- avoid using phrases or information which date the leaflet (unless it has only a very short life-span).

It may be useful to read Chapter 5, Writing to be Read.

It is essential to:

- state who has issued the leaflet or brochure
- include a name, address and telephone number so that readers can obtain more information
- check and double-check the contents.

Writing by committee is inefficient and usually non-productive. It is easier and faster for one person to prepare a draft and then obtain comments from the other people involved. Once the draft has been completed, it should be shown to two or three other people who have not taken part in the drafting and who, preferably, have no links with the subject of the document. From their different perspectives, they may spot gaps or mistakes which have escaped the authors.

This is the time to start thinking, with the graphic designer, about any illustrations. If photographs or plans are to be used, they have to be selected. If nothing suitable exists, photographs will have to be taken and plans drawn – all in time to meet the production schedule.

Production

With the design approved, text written and the illustrations ready, the leaflet or brochure will take shape in the form of artwork. Traditionally, the designer had the text typeset to fit the layout and assembled all the material on a flat board ready for the printer. The artwork would be in black and white, but marked to show where coloured areas would appear. Today, it is more likely that the artwork will be produced on a computer and a floppy disk supplied to the printer.

The client must ensure that all stages of the work are thoroughly checked – and checked again. It is vital that the original text you supply to the graphic designer or printer has been checked word by word and comma by comma. Corrections afterwards are expensive.

Most health service organizations have word processors with a range of typefaces. The typesetting stage can therefore be by-passed by providing a floppy disk of the text, which the designer or printer can then use or convert to fit the layout. In that way, both the cost and the likelihood of errors are reduced.

Nevertheless, the client should check the artwork for any wrongly positioned paragraphs or pages and ensure that the printer knows where any illustrations should go.

If a commercial printer is being used, all the necessary specifications will have been drawn up in advance with the graphic designer. Managers have only to ensure that the production schedule and delivery date are agreed and can be met, and that precise delivery instructions (name, address, and telephone and fax numbers) have been provided.

If a large quantity of the publication will be needed, it is a false economy to print half now and half in the next financial year. It costs much more to put the work back onto the machines than to complete the job in one print run. On the other hand, it pays not to be over-enthu-siastic in ordering: managers should assess their needs realistically.

When cost is a critical factor, or the project is a small one, it may be possible to produce the leaflet or brochure in-house without using graphic designers or printers. The development of desk top publish-ing (DTP) has brought production within reach of many health service organizations. A combination of DTP equipment, a photocopier, laser printer, coloured paper and simple design can create a leaflet which is attractive and has impact.

In-house production may save money on design and typesetting, but, in costing this kind of production, managers should include staff time (including any finishing, folding and stapling which may be needed) and consider the 'knock-on' effect which production will have on the work of reprographic staff.

Quantity and quality are crucial factors. Even the best in-house printing and production equipment may have technical limitations and be unable to match the capacity and standards of work done com-mercially.

Distribution

With a large quantity of leaflets or brochures, distribution can be a major problem. Points to be considered include:

- storage – if the leaflets or brochures are to be used over a long period, they should be stored in a warm and dry place

- internal distribution – can the internal post cope? Can managers at unit or ward level, for example, ensure that leaflets meant for all staff will actually reach them? Should they be sent with pay-slips, perhaps? Should advance copies be sent to anyone connected with the project?

- outside circulation – lists of addresses of people or organizations who need to see the leaflet or brochure should be prepared

- mass distribution – if door-to-door distribution is needed, local voluntary organizations with an interest in the subject may be able to help.

GLOSSARY OF DESIGNERS' AND PRINTERS' TERMS

Designers and printers have their own jargon and buzz-words. Some of the most commonly used terms are explained below.

Authors' corrections (A/Cs) Changes the client makes to **proofs** or **artwork** which are other than errors made by the supplier. Often seen on invoices because they are the responsibility of the client and therefore chargeable to him or her.

Artwork The material from which a printer makes plates.

Bromide A photographic print used in the production of **artwork** (see **PMT**).

Cromalin or **Matchprint** A type of **proof** made from the **colour separations** just before making plates for printing. A photographic technique which, though not 100% accurate, provides an excellent final check.

Colour In printing, the number of colours relates to the number of colours put on the paper by the machine. The colour of the paper does not count: for example, a job with black and red text on a yellow paper is a two-colour job.

Colour separations Part of the **origination** process where colour pictures and **artwork** are broken down into the four process colours – cyan, yellow, magenta and black – and a separate piece of film is made for each one to make a set of printing plates.

Concept The original or underlying design idea.

Copy The text of a document, either supplied by the client or written by a copywriter.

Cym Short for cyan, yellow, magenta. A way of specifying colour. In full-colour work, all colours are made up from dots of these colours and black. On **artwork** you may see a colour specified as 100% cyan, 50% yellow and 5% magenta.

Desk top publishing (DTP) Most design today is carried out on computer – the Apple Macintosh being the industry standard – and DTP programs such as PageMaker and QuarkXpress are used. This brings considerable cost savings, particularly where client's **copy** is supplied on floppy disk.

Gsm Short for grams per square metre. Used to signify weights of paper or board. Text pages may be about 135 gsm to 170 gsm. Cover boards may be 230 gsm to 350 gsm.

Half-tone A term used for photographs in printed documents.

Library pic A photograph from a commercial picture library, for which a reproduction fee must be paid.

Logo Short for 'logotype', a combination of letters and/or words, and a symbol or motif, arranged in a distinctive style. Often used as part of a corporate 'signature', such as NHS Executive, Coca-Cola, BBC, Kellogg's and ICI.

Mark-up The instructions to a printer or plate maker written on the **artwork** by the designer.

Origination The work done by a plate maker or **repro house** to make the material from which a printer can produce the printed job. For a full-colour job on a short print run, this may be the largest cost element.

Page One printed side of a sheet of paper. Hence, a single piece of A4 paper printed on both sides would be a two-page document. A piece of A4 paper folded in half and printed on each face would be an A5, four-page (4 pp) document.

Pantone or **PMS** A matching system for colour mixing. Designers will often specify a colour such as PMS 185. Swatch books are available showing the complete range of available colours and **tints**.

PMT Short for photo-mechanical transfer, otherwise known as a **bromide**. This is a photographic print made from a piece of **artwork** or other matter to be supplied to a printer for publication. The production of one piece of **artwork** may require the use of a number of PMTs of **text**, **logos**, or illustrations.

pp Short for pages, as in 48 pp.

Proof Produced at various stages for the client's approval. They may be laser-proofs of **text** alone or layouts. At later stages they may be proofs of **artwork**. Finally, they will be proofs of the plates prior to printing. They should always be carefully checked. The earlier the stage at which corrections are made, the less they cost.

Repro house A company which specializes in making film and plates which a printer uses to print colour material.

Rules Straight lines used in documents.

Run-on (R/O) An additional quantity of a document produced at the same time as the main run. Often used for quoting purposes. A price of £1000 for 5000, plus £75 per 1000 R/O, means that if 7000 are ordered, the price will be £1150. Not to be confused with a reprint, which takes place later, as a separate operation, and will therefore cost more than the run-on price.

Saddle-stitched Stapled.

Scamp A quick **visual**.

Scan The job a plate maker does to turn a photograph into an image made of dots which can be printed. Scans are quite expensive and the cost of a colour document will vary according to their number and size.

Screen When a photograph is converted to dots to allow it to be printed, the size and closeness of the dots are determined by a 'screen' of lines crossing each other at 90°. The size is described in lines per inch or centimetre. Newsprint photographs require a coarser screen than those printed on art paper.

Self-cover A document where the cover is printed on the same kind and weight of material as the **text**.

Serif The fine line, or squiggly bit, projecting from the main stroke of a printed letter or number. **Sans serif** describes a character without the squiggly bit. An example of a serif typeface is Times, often used for newspaper text. Helvetica is a sans serif typeface, commonly used for signs.

Stock Paper and board. This includes art paper, coated with china clay for excellent colour reproduction. The papers may be matt or gloss.

Text The pages of a document as distinct from the cover.

Tint A pale version of colour created by breaking it down into small dots. By varying the size (percentage) of these dots a range of intensities can be achieved, from 5% (almost white) to 100% (the original solid colour).

Typography The skill of a designer in the selection, specification and layout of type to fit and be appropriate to the document, and be readable and attractive.

Typesetting The job of turning **copy** into **text** which can be printed. The job of 'keyboarding', physically typing in the **copy**, has been reduced by the use of **DTP** programs which can read the client's floppy disk.

Upper and lower (U/L) Capital and small letters. Small letters are lower case; capitals are upper case.

Visual A mock-up or representation of a finished design produced by a designer to show to the client.

8

Research and evaluation

Lord Forte is credited with saying: 'I am sure we waste half of the money we spend on advertising. The problem is we don't know which half.'

Health service managers and public relations practitioners have to make sure they are not similarly baffled when investing public money in public relations effort. They have a responsibility to ensure it is not wasted. One way is through research and evaluation.

WHAT RESEARCH AND EVALUATION ACHIEVE

Research and evaluation will not only help you spend wisely. They will:

1 encourage you to set clear performance goals for public relations effort

2 help you to adjust campaign or programme planning to ensure it achieves its goals

3 enable you to monitor the effectiveness of different techniques and so learn from both your successes and your mistakes

4 help to demonstrate value for money which, in turn, helps to develop consent and commitment throughout the organization

5 demonstrate the contribution of public relations to the overall objectives of the organization.

Setting performance goals

Public relations performance goals can take many forms. Examples are:

• to improve the take-up of a particular service

- to win acceptance for a new form of service delivery
- to improve recruitment and/or retention of staff
- to build a positive public image in a particular target audience
- to influence particular legislation or decisions.

But, while these are useful headers, they are not the finished product. The performance goal in a public relations strategy document that says, 'Our major aim must be to raise public awareness of developments within the trust', raises more questions than it answers: Why? Among whom? Which developments? What do we want them to know? How many know it now? How many will know it after our public relations intervention? And so on.

Performance goals for public relations activities need to be established before the public relations activity occurs, not afterwards. They must be clear and measurable, and they must be clearly linked to the overall strategic objectives of the organization.

Some public relations activities are difficult to evaluate because they lack coherent goals from the outset.

Adjustments to campaign planning

If evaluation procedures are sufficiently responsive, it is often possible to detect whether the strategy is working and, if not, where it is going wrong. This will allow you to make adjustments as you go and to maintain your performance goals.

An example of this kind of monitoring is as follows:

Question 1: Are we reaching the designated target audience with our communications?
If no: Find out why and make adjustments. If yes: Move on to Question 2.

Question 2: Is the target audience receiving our key message from our communications?
If no: Find out why and make adjustments. If yes: Move on to Question 3.

Question 3: Is the target audience responding in the way we wish?
If no: Find out why and make adjustments. If yes: Move on to Question 4.

Question 4: Which restaurant shall we hold our celebration in?!

Monitoring the effectiveness of different communications techniques

If your evaluation procedures are adequate, they should show:

- whether the defined target audiences are receiving the key messages, and
- how they are receiving the key messages.

From this information, the health service manager and public relations practitioner will learn that some techniques work well with some target audiences and that others do not. If they discover that leaflets do not work with a particular target audience they have not wasted money; they have learned something that will save money in the future.

In this respect, senior managers have a responsibility to think before they shoot the messenger when anything goes wrong. If that is all they do, no-one will ever admit that a particular technique has not worked, and the organization will never learn from its mistakes.

Demonstrating value for money

Public relations practitioners must submit their work to the kind of scrutiny that develops understanding of their contribution, and ultimately enhances its value. The tendency to 'hide' the costs of particular public relations activities among other costs is a recipe for unrealistic expectations of what public relations can do, and of the costs required to do it. Health authority and trust boards and other senior decision-makers are more likely to value public relations if they know what it really costs and achieves, and can see clearly the relationship between public relations outcomes and strategic objectives.

Demonstrating the contribution of public relations to the overall objectives of the organization

Public relations activities are not a law unto themselves. Public relations must be seen as a strategic activity and not as press releases plus a bit of crisis management. It is the responsibility of board members to identify clear strategic objectives for the organization they manage, and it is the responsibility of public relations practitioners to demonstrate the strategic value of their contribution. They will do this only by linking their work to coherent outcomes which serve organizational objectives.

Some public relations practitioners claim that public relations cannot be evaluated. The proposition is a dangerous one. Certainly, it is not particularly easy to evaluate public relations, but health service managers are increasingly demanding evidence that a technique works before they will fund it. This is true of patient care, and must be even more so in the case of public relations.

RESEARCH AND EVALUATION METHODS

Evaluation should not be an optional process bolted on to the very end of a campaign. It should be considered from the outset. It may indeed provide a good focus for determining clear objectives and realistic and tangible outcomes.

A major part of the evaluation process will entail research:

- to determine the nature of the need at the outset

- to validate and shape the strategy chosen to meet the need

- to demonstrate the final outcome.

Market research

One way of building up a picture about the nature of the need at the outset of, say, a public relations campaign is to conduct some market research. Market research is the systematic gathering, recording, analysis and interpretation of information to guide the decision-making process.

Health services are depicted by the Government as more responsive to consumer needs than ever before, a premise that underlines a need for a dialogue between health care providers and consumers. 'Gut instinct' probably suggests how consumers feel about particular issues, but this needs to be verified objectively. Market research can help you to do that.

There are two basic kinds of research: quantitative and qualitative. Quantitative research will tell you how many people are happy or unhappy about an issue. Qualitative research will help you understand why.

Quantitative research is often conducted by self-completion questionnaires. It is important that these are straightforward and unambiguous. The value of this form of research is to produce evidence of a weight of opinion, although the validity of a self-selecting sample must always be considered critically. If a depth of understanding is needed, then qualitative research is more appropriate.

Qualitative research elicits feelings and attitudes. It is descriptive and anecdotal in form, and is generally conducted face-to-face, with the interviewer working through a series of question areas on a 'topic guide'.

In some circumstances, you may need both quantitative and qualitative research in order to gain not only an understanding about current perceptions but also an indication of the weight of opinion. Whichever form you choose, you must be clear about what you hope to learn from the research.

There is no single way to evaluate all public relations activities. Indeed, different activities may call for different evaluation techniques. The rest of this chapter gives some broad approaches which can be developed and adapted to individual circumstances.

Benchmark research

There are many circumstances in which you will need to establish benchmarks. If, for instance, you intend to use public relations activities to stimulate greater use by the local community of a particular health care facility, useful benchmarks might be:

- What percentage of the target audience is aware of the facility at the outset of the campaign?

- What percentage of them makes use of it at the outset?

At the completion of the campaign, you can re-assess these factors and see how many more members of the target audience are aware of the facility and how many more are using it. This information will allow you to establish a unit cost per extra user of the facility and thus find out whether the effort made has been cost-efficient or not.

Benchmarks can be established in various ways, such as telephone research, postal questionnaires, street interviews, and discussion groups. They are useful in attempting to bring about a change in awareness, attitude or behaviour. Behaviour is often the crucial quality criteria for public relations campaigns. If 20% more people know about the facility after the campaign, but no more people are using it, not a lot has been achieved.

However, even if more people are using the facility, it is still necessary to identify why. The reasons may have nothing to do with the public relations campaign! It is possible to delude oneself about the effectiveness of the public relations techniques used – and to fail in the next campaign as a result.

Benchmark research has its limitations. One of them is that it tends to tell you only *after* the event whether you have succeeded or not. Obviously, in longer-term projects, it is useful to know before it ends how successful the campaign is proving. In that way, data gained from the evaluation process can be used to make adjustments to the campaign as it unfolds. This approach allows the campaigners to learn as they go and can avoid mistakes that are both costly and time-consuming. This calls for tracking research.

Tracking research

Tracking research can be used to identify the same kinds of information as benchmark research. In the campaign to promote more use of a particular health care facility, tracking research can show how many people know about it and how many use it. Because the results are tracked throughout the campaign, they will also show how things are developing before the end of the process.

Tracking research is particularly useful where a perceptual or attitudinal shift is needed in the target audience. The use of discussion groups (sometimes called focus groups) enables you to monitor shifts and establish their origins.

Organizations committed to proactive public relations often use tracking research to monitor changing attitudes to the organization. In that way, the strategic planning of public relations can be based on up-to-date information about attitudinal shifts in target audiences.

Evaluating media relations

A traditional way to evaluate media work is to estimate column inches published or quantity of words broadcast. In sophisticated models, the coverage is categorized as negative, neutral or positive.

More complex models of evaluation are based on the weighting of certain factors against others. Among the factors that can be used are:

- total reach
- target audience reach
- impact achieved
- delivery of key messages
- cost effectiveness.

Total reach is the potential audience reached by a piece of coverage. This is arrived at by establishing the audience, not the circulation, and excludes incidental coverage.

Target audience reach is an estimation of the reach among key target audiences.

Impact achieved is related to factors that add impact, such as size, location in the newspaper, exclusivity, and illustrations or photographs, quotes and headlines.

Delivery of key messages is an estimation of the extent to which the coverage has reflected the key messages the organization wished to convey.

Cost effectiveness is cost divided by the reach. Comparisons can be made with other means of communication and costs of previous campaigns.

Evaluating events

This is another area that is difficult to evaluate. Factors that can be used include:

- numbers of the target audience who attended
- publicity generated
- audience response
- number of audience responses made after the event
- cost effectiveness.

Evaluating lobbying activities

When dealing with politicians, it is wise not to rely too much on what they say; look instead at what they do. Are they using information you have provided in speeches, documents or papers of their own? Are they suggesting other politicians who might be sympathetic to your point of view? Are they using your arguments in debate? Are they putting forward your ideas? Are they voting the way you would hope?

Evaluating crisis management

Testing your crisis management procedures should form part of the procedures themselves. So when the real thing happens, look at:

- media impact
- positive/negative balance
- effects on residual image
- rate of image recovery.

LAST BUT NOT LEAST...

This has been the last chapter of *Health Service Public Relations*. But evaluation should not be the last thing to be done in public relations work. The traditional planning route for public relations remains:

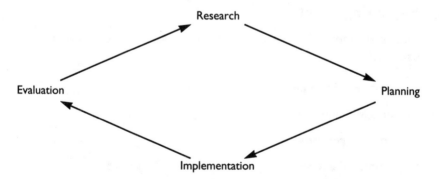

Public relations practice is the 'planned and sustained effort to establish and maintain goodwill and mutual understanding between an organization and its public' (Institute of Public Relations). Evaluation and re-evaluation are essential components of it.

The National Association of Health Service Public Relations Officers

The National Association of Health Service Public Relations Officers (NAHSPRO) exists to:

- encourage and enable communications and public relations staff working in the health service to share knowledge, experience and skills

- spread recognition of the valuable contribution of professional public relations skills in the health service

- improve the standard of public relations practice in the health service

- provide appropriate public relations training.

Membership ranges from public relations managers and press officers in trusts and district and family health services authorities to senior communications specialists at national level. Through associate membership, the Association embraces the skills of freelances and public relations consultants.

Index